POSITIVE AFFIRMATIONS JOURNAL FOR BLACK TEEN BOYS

3 SIMPLE STEPS TO EFFECTIVELY USE AFFIRMATIONS TO IMPROVE YOUR SELF-ESTEEM, MOTIVATION, AND CONFIDENCE

B. MITCHELL-DOS SANTOS

DISCLAIMER

Hey there, amazing teenagers!

Before diving into this positive affirmation book, journal, and guide, I want to make sure you're aware of a few essential things. Firstly, while positive affirmations can be an incredibly powerful tool for improving your mindset and self-confidence, they are not a replacement for professional help. If you're struggling with mental health issues, it's important to seek the support of a licensed therapist or healthcare professional.

Secondly, the information in this book is intended for educational purposes only. While I've done my best to provide accurate and up-to-date information, I do not guarantee that the information presented in this book is complete, correct, or suitable for your needs.

Finally, please remember that the success of positive affirmations depends on your willingness to practice them regularly and believe in their power. Results may vary, and it's essential to be patient and consistent in your practice.

With that said, I'm so excited for you to explore the world of positive affirmations and start using them to transform your life! Let's do this together! Remember to approach this journey with an open mind and a willingness to learn and grow.

CONTENTS

INTRODUCTION

Did you know that a recent global research study conducted in 2022 found that teenagers spend a whopping 9 hours and 22 minutes per day on screens and consuming media? That's a lot of time, right? This includes time spent on smartphones, computers, tablets, TVs, and other digital devices.

I get it - screens are a huge part of our lives. We use our smartphones for everything from messaging our friends to ordering food, and TV shows are just so darn addictive.

But here's the thing - excessive screen time and media consumption can seriously negatively affect your mental and physical health. Poor sleep quality decreased physical activity, and an increased risk of anxiety and depression are just a few examples. That's why it's essential to ensure you're taking breaks from your screens and finding other ways to stay active and engaged.

As a teenager, you're going through many changes and facing various challenges that can impact your self-esteem and confidence. But I want you to know that you're not alone in this. This book was written to equip you with the needed tools and resources to help you overcome these challenges and build a positive mindset. You've got this!

I understand your pain when it comes to staying away from social media and screen use. It can be challenging to break away from the constant scrolling and notifications you get now and then, especially when you feel like you're missing out on something important. But the truth is excessive screen time can significantly impact your mental and physical health.

Breaking away from the screen is tough, but giving your the screen is tough, but giving your brain and body a break is important. Believe me; it's worth it in the long run.

One of the most common side effects you will experience when you are exposed to too much screen time at a tender age is eye strain and headaches. Staring at a screen for prolonged periods can cause your eyes to become dry and irritated, leading to discomfort and pain. This can make it difficult to focus on other tasks or even get a good night's sleep.

In addition to physical discomfort, the constant use of social media and screen use can negatively impact your mental health while growing up. It can also contribute to anxiety and depression because you will feel pressured to present a perfect image of yourself among your peers. If care is not taken, you start comparing yourself to others online, leading to feelings of inadequacy and low self-esteem.

As a teenager, it's important to recognize that too much access to social media can contribute to the **perpetuation** of racism and discrimination in our society. The images and messages we see on social media, television, and other forms of media can reinforce negative **stereotypes** about African Americans and impact the way that the majority of society views Black people.

Furthermore, social media can be a tool for hate speech and online harassment. Racists and **bigots** can use social media platforms to spread hateful messages and target individuals or groups based on race or ethnicity, severely impacting you as a teenager.

Imagine a future where you are empowered with confidence, motivation, and higher self-esteem. A future where you are comfortable in your own skin and believe in your ability to achieve your goals and aspirations.

In this future, you will no longer feel pressured to **conform** to societal expectations. Instead, you will grow to embrace your unique qualities and celebrate your individuality. You will be free to express yourself among your peers authentically and creatively without fear of judgment or rejection.

It may seem like a far-off dream, but getting there is possible. It takes time, effort, and some serious self-love, but trust me, it's worth it. So keep working towards your goals, and don't be afraid to be yourself.

In our **fast-paced** and often stressful world, it's easy to get caught up in self-doubt and negative self-talk. But with the help of this book on positive affirmations guide and journal, you can change your mindset and quickly achieve your goals.

Hey teens! Listen up, 'cause I've got something important to tell you. Half the battle is in your head when it comes to achieving your dreams. Yup, that's right! Doubts can creep in and mess with your head, telling you that you're not good enough, smart enough, or capable enough because you see your friends doing way better than you... you get the drift. But let me tell you something - if you've got a dream burning in your heart, it is possible!

Don't let those doubts get the best of you.

Instead, try telling yourself some positive things. These will give you the confidence and motivation you need to take action and chase after your dreams. Trust me; it's just as easy to believe in yourself as it is to doubt yourself. So go on, replace those negative thoughts with empowering ones. Believe in yourself and go out there and make it happen!

This book is not just a list of positive affirmations but a journal and guide to personalize the affirmations and take positive actions.

Are you wondering what's in it for you if you read this book? Let me tell you; there's a whole lot to gain! Here are just a few examples:

This is a BIG deal, folks. First, you'll learn how to transform those negative thoughts into positive ones. By swapping out negative self-talk for uplifting affirmations, you'll start to see the world and yourself in a brighter, more positive light.

Secondly, you'll boost your self-esteem. Positive affirmations can help you believe in yourself and your abilities, giving you the confidence to take on new challenges and succeed in school and life.

Thirdly, you'll say goodbye to stress and anxiety. Negative thoughts can be a real downer, and they can cause some significant anxiety. But with positive affirmations, you'll learn how to manage those thoughts and feelings in a healthy way. Say hello to a more relaxed and positive outlook on life!

Fourthly, you'll develop resilience. Life can be challenging, and we all face obstacles from time to time. But with the power of positive affirmations, you'll learn how to bounce back from setbacks and keep pushing forward. This resilience will help you tackle anything life throws your way.

Last but not least, you'll build better relationships. Positive affirmations can help you cultivate a more positive attitude toward yourself and others. When you positively approach the world, you'll attract more positive people into your life and build stronger, healthier relationships.

So there you have it, folks! This book is packed with many benefits that will help you become the best version of yourself. What are you waiting for? Dive in and start reaping the rewards!

Get ready to unlock the power of positive affirmations with me. In this book, I will share some seriously effective techniques that can help you boost your confidence and improve your self-image.

No matter what you're struggling with, whether it's low self-esteem or negative self-talk, positive affirmations can help. By learning the right strategies, you can use positive affirmations to overcome those limiting beliefs and build self-confidence. Trust me; you deserve to be happy and successful. Positive affirmations can help you get there.

As a vibrant mother of 3 young black boys, I understand the importance of building self-esteem in young children, especially in a world that can be so negative and critical. That's why I've made positive affirmations a part of my children's daily routine, and it's been incredibly effective in boosting their self-confidence and empowering them to pursue their dreams.

So, if you're ready to level up and start feeling amazing, then let's do this together! I'm here to guide you every step of the way. Let's go! Are you ready?

CHAPTER ONE

EFFECTS OF MEDIA ON TEENS

Great to see you again! We're diving into the next chapter of this book, and I can't wait to take you on a journey exploring the impact of media on teenagers. Let's get started and learn more together!

Have you ever stopped to think about how much the media we consume shapes our perceptions of ourselves and others? It's crazy to think about, but it's true. The images, messages, and stories we see and hear in the media can significantly impact how we see ourselves and the people around us.

Let's start with the good stuff. Media can be a great way to learn about new things, communicate and connect with people. Whether talking to friends who live far away or meeting new people who share your interests, media can help you form meaningful connections and easily communicate. It can also be a platform for self-expression, allowing you to share your thoughts, feelings, and creativity with others.

Media can also be a source of information and education. You can learn about new topics, follow your favorite experts and influencers, and even take courses online. Plus, social media can be a great way to stay up-to-date on current events and news.

Unfortunately, media isn't all rainbows and butterflies. One of the media's most significant adverse effects on teenagers is its potential impact on mental health. Studies have shown that excessive media, such as television, serve as a possible negative factor in the racial identity development of modern teenagers, causing feelings of anxiety, depression, and loneliness. Comparing yourself to others online can also be damaging to self-esteem and confidence.

In addition to mental health concerns, physical health risks are associated with media. Sitting for long periods while using the media can lead to a sedentary lifestyle and health problems such as obesity and poor posture.

It breaks my heart to say that cyberbullying is a significant issue affecting many teenagers today. It can be as damaging to mental health as in-person bullying and have long-lasting effects.

That's not to say that technology is all bad. There are many benefits to staying connected and using online resources to learn and grow. But it's essential to find a healthy balance and be mindful of how much time we spend in front of screens.

You know, there's been a lot of talk lately about the negative impacts of social media. But I think it's important to remember that there are also some great benefits to staying connected online.

For one thing, social media allows us to stay in touch with family and friends no matter where we are in the world. Whether through messaging, video calls, or sharing photos and updates, we can keep up with the people we care about, even when we're miles apart.

Another great benefit of social media is the support networks it can provide. Whether it's finding a community of people who share similar interests or connecting with others going through a similar experience, social media can be a valuable source of comfort and encouragement.

And let's not forget about the wealth of information available online. Social media can be a great way to learn and grow, from news and current events to educational resources and tutorials.

Remember, this book was written to help you navigate the ups and downs of media, including dealing with cyberbullying. So let's work together to create a safer and kinder online community!

Television Media as a Potential Negative Factor in the Racial Identity Development of Teenagers

Hey there, teenager! Let's talk about something that might make you mad: the portrayal of racial **stereotypes** in media. It's a big problem, and it affects all of us. It might not be something you've thought about, but it's a big part of who you are.

You've probably seen it yourself - how certain races are portrayed in movies, TV shows, and even commercials. Maybe you've seen a character who's the "funny" sidekick or the "angry" person who's always causing trouble. These stereotypes are harmful because they reduce people to caricatures and can lead to prejudice and discrimination.

Seeing these stereotypes in the media can affect how you see people in real life. You might start to believe that certain races are "funny" or "angry" all the time, even though that's not true. This can lead to many problems, like discrimination, bullying, and even violence.

It's no secret that television media has a significant impact on teenagers. Unfortunately, much of this impact is negative. Television often promotes unrealistic beauty standards that can mess with your self-esteem as a teenager. You know those shows where everyone looks perfect all the time? Yeah, those aren't doing anyone any favors. They can make you feel like you're not good enough as a teenager, leading to issues like anxiety and depression.

But it's not just beauty standards that are the problem. Television also tends to portray a lot of racial stereotypes that can be damaging to young people. When teens see certain races portrayed negatively, it can lead to prejudice and discrimination (Martin, Ardis C. 2008).

And let's not forget about television's impact on a teen's social life. When they see certain behaviors or attitudes on TV, they might start to think that those things are normal or even desirable. This can lead to all sorts of problems with peer groups, which is something that nobody wants.

Let's take a good look at this example, shall we?

Let's talk about something significant: racism and discrimination. Unfortunately, these issues continue to be a problem in our society, affecting people of all races and backgrounds. One group that is particularly impacted by racism and discrimination is African Americans, and the media plays a significant role in perpetuating negative stereotypes and attitudes toward them.

When we watch TV shows, movies, or news broadcasts, we're often exposed to images and messages reinforcing harmful stereotypes about African Americans. We might see them portrayed as criminals, lazy, or uneducated. These images can be damaging for African Americans and everyone in society (Martin, Artis C. 2008).

The problem with these stereotypes is that they create a false narrative about African Americans, and it can be hard to change people's perceptions once they've been formed. Even if we don't consciously believe these negative messages, they can still impact our unconscious biases and the way we interact with people in our daily lives.

Your racial identity is all about how you see yourself and your place in the world in relation to your race or ethnicity. It's shaped by things like your family background, community, and experiences growing up.

Developing a solid racial identity is crucial because it helps you feel connected to your culture and heritage. It can also give you a sense of pride and belonging that's important for your emotional well-being.

But here's the thing: developing a strong racial identity isn't always easy, especially when you're a teenager. You might feel pressure to fit in with your friends or to downplay your cultural background to avoid being different.

That's why knowing how media can shape our attitudes toward race is important. If we're not careful, we might believe that certain races are "better" or "worse" than others because that's what we've seen in the media.

Being proud of who you are and where you come from can give you the strength to stand up for yourself and others who share your culture. It can also help you form meaningful connections with people who understand and appreciate your background.

So if you haven't thought much about your racial identity, now is a great time to start. Talk to your family about your heritage, learn about the history of your culture, and seek out opportunities to connect with other people who share your background.

When you see a stereotype in the media, call it out. Talk to your friends and family about why it's harmful, and encourage them to see people as individuals rather than stereotypes.

It's essential to recognize that racism and discrimination aren't just individual problems. They're also systemic issues built into our institutions and cultural narratives. So, what can you do about it as a teenager?

First, you can start by being aware of the media you consume and how it portrays African Americans. You can ask yourself questions like, "Is this image or message reinforcing a harmful stereotype?" or "How would you feel if you were in the shoes of the person being portrayed in this way?" By being mindful of what you see and hear, you can challenge your biases and work towards a more inclusive and equitable society.

So many amazing artists, writers, and activists are doing vital work to challenge stereotypes and promote positive narratives about African Americans. By supporting their work and sharing their messages, you can help to shift the cultural narrative and create a more just and equitable society for everyone. You can also seek out media that portray African Americans in a positive and empowering way.

Seek out books, movies, and TV shows that celebrate diversity and show people from diverse backgrounds in a positive light. You can also support media that portrays different races positively and realistically. By supporting this kind of media, you're sending a message that representation matters and that you won't stand for harmful stereotypes.

Remember, your racial identity is an important part of who you are and is something to be proud of. Embrace it, celebrate it, and let it help you become the best version of yourself!

Remember, you have the power to change the narrative. By speaking up and supporting media that celebrates diversity, you can help create a world where people are valued for who they are, not reduced to harmful stereotypes.

So, let's take a stand against racism and discrimination and work towards a more inclusive and equitable society. Let's challenge harmful stereotypes and celebrate the diversity that makes our communities and our world so amazing. Let's do this together! We all have a role to play in creating a better future; together, we can make it happen.

Teens and Social Media Use: A Closer Look at the Impact on Teens

In this section, we'll discuss something that's probably a big part of your life – Social media. As a teenager, you're likely spending a lot of time scrolling through various social media platforms. While there are definitely some good things about social media, there are also some negative aspects that you should be aware of.

I recently read a pretty eye-opening statistic: 79% of teens used social media and online videos at least once a week. And get this - 32% said they "wouldn't want to live without" YouTube! That's a pretty big statement if you ask me (Riehm KE et al., 2019).

But it's not just teens who are glued to their screens. Nearly two-thirds of tweens watch TV, 64% watch online videos, and 43% play games on a smartphone or tablet every single day. That's a lot of screen time, guys.

So what does all of this mean? Well, it's no secret that technology has become a massive part of our lives. We use it to stay connected with friends, learn new things, and entertain ourselves. But too much screen time can have some negative consequences, especially when it comes to our mental health.

❖ **The Good, The Bad, and The Ugly: Understanding the Impact of Social Media on Teens.**

Have you ever stopped to think about how social media has changed the way we communicate and connect with each other? It's pretty impressive but also a bit complicated.

Social media is everywhere these days, and it's hard to escape its impact on our lives. Some of it is good, some of it is bad, and some of it is just downright ugly. But what does that all mean for us as teenagers?

Let's start with the good. Social media allows us to connect with people from all over the world, share our interests and hobbies, and learn new things. We can follow our favorite musicians, actors, and athletes and get a behind-the-scenes look at their lives. We can join online communities that share our passions and find support and encouragement when needed.

But there's also a darker side to social media. Cyberbullying, for example, is a real problem that affects many teens. It's easy to hide behind a screen and say hurtful things to others, and social media platforms can sometimes feel like a breeding ground for negativity and hate. And then there's the issue of addiction - it's so easy to get sucked into the endless scrolling, liking, and commenting that we can lose track of time and neglect our real-life relationships.

Also, social media can make it harder to connect with others truly. We've all experienced the frustration of sending a message, posting a comment, and not getting a response. Plus, it's easy to misinterpret tone and intent online - what might seem like a harmless joke to one person can be hurtful to another. We can feel like we're shouting into the void, and nobody is listening.

So, what's the ugly part of social media? Well, it's the way that it can warp our perceptions of ourselves and others. We're bombarded with images of "perfect" bodies, lifestyles, and relationships, and it can be easy to feel like we're not measuring up. We can start comparing ourselves to others and feeling inadequate, leading to anxiety, depression, and other mental health issues.

Studies have shown that spending too much time on social media can lead to feelings of anxiety, depression, and low self-esteem. It can also impact our ability to sleep, which can have a ripple effect on our overall health and well-being.

A 2019 study of more than 500 12-15 yr old's in the US found that those who spent more than 3 hours per day using social media might be at a higher risk for internalizing problems. (internalizing can involve social withdrawal, difficulty coping with anxiety or depression, or directing feelings inward) (Woods HC et al., 2016).

The bottom line is that social media can be a powerful tool for good, but we must be aware of its potential pitfalls. We must use it mindfully and not let it control our lives. Let's focus on building real, meaningful connections with others both online and offline, and remember that our worth isn't determined by the number of likes or followers we have.

❖ **Navigating Online Relationships: Building Connections and Staying Safe on Social Media.**

Online relationships can be great, but being aware of the potential risks and staying safe on social media is essential.

Firstly, remember that not everyone you meet online is who they say they are. People can easily create fake profiles and pretend to be someone else. Be cautious when talking to strangers online, and don't share any personal information until you feel comfortable and confident that they are who they say they are.

Secondly, be careful about the information you share online. Don't post personal details such as your address or phone number; be wary of sharing intimate photos or videos. Remember, once you post something online, it's out there forever.

Thirdly, be aware of the signs of online grooming or cyberbullying. If someone makes you feel uncomfortable or is harassing you online, don't engage with them and report them to the relevant authorities or social media platforms.

Finally, always trust your gut. If something feels off or too good to be true, it probably is. Don't be afraid to talk to a trusted adult or seek support if you feel unsure about an online relationship or situation.

Remember, social media can be a great way to connect with others, but be aware of the potential risks and stay safe. Let's focus on building positive relationships and spreading kindness online!

❖ **Mindful Social Media Use: Establishing a Healthy Balance and Avoiding the Pitfalls.**

Social media has become a huge part of our lives, but as a teenager, use it mindfully and establish a healthy balance. It's easy to get sucked into endless scrolling, liking, and commenting, but this can lead to neglecting our real-life relationships and responsibilities.

So, what can we do to practice mindful social media use?

Firstly, set boundaries for yourself. Decide how much time you want to spend on social media daily, and stick to it. Turn off notifications so you're not constantly being pulled back in.

Secondly, be aware of social media's impact on your mental health. If you feel anxious or depressed after spending time on social media, take a break and focus on something else that makes you feel good.

Thirdly, be mindful of the content you consume and share. It's important to remember that not everything you see on social media is true or accurate. Try to fact-check before sharing anything, and avoid spreading harmful messages.

Finally, don't let social media define your worth. Your value as a person is not determined by the number of likes or followers you have. Remember to focus on building real, meaningful online and offline connections with others.

Social media can be a powerful tool, but use it mindfully and establish a healthy balance in your life. Let's focus on staying connected with others while prioritizing our mental health and well-being.

So, let's take a step back and consider our technology use. Are we spending too much time on social media or watching videos? Are we feeling anxious or stressed because of it? If so, it might be time to take a break and focus on some other activities that bring us joy and fulfillment.

Remember, guys - technology is a tool, but it's up to us to use it in a way that supports our well-being and happiness. Let's make sure we're using it in a positive and fulfilling way and not letting it take over our lives.

So, next time you're scrolling through Instagram or chatting with friends on Snapchat, take a moment to appreciate the benefits of social media. It's not all bad - there's much to be grateful for. Let's use technology to build meaningful connections, learn new things, and make the most of all the fantastic resources available to us.

How can you defend yourself as a teenager against the negative influences that can lead to low self-esteem, a poor sense of self, and high anxiety? And how can you find the motivation and confidence to become your best self? These are essential questions that many teenagers struggle with daily. The answer lies in positive self-affirmations, which provide us with the defensive tools we need to transform negative thoughts into positive ones.

In the next chapter, we will explore the power of self-affirmation and how it can help you combat these negative inputs and develop a strong and positive sense of self.

Let's dive into chapter 2 to learn more about the power of self-affirmation and how it can help us build a stronger sense of self.

CHAPTER TWO

THE SCIENCE BEHIND SELF-AFFIRMATIONS

Hey again, teenagers! Today we're going to talk about a topic that might change how you think about yourself: self-affirmations. You may have heard of them before, but do you know what they are and how they work? We're going to dive into the science behind self-affirmations and explore how they can help you build confidence, overcome self-doubt, and achieve your goals.

Let's quickly talk about something important - how we see ourselves.

You know that feeling when you've worked really hard on something, and then someone criticizes it? It can feel pretty bad, right? That's because we're all motivated to protect how we see ourselves and our worth.

It's like we all have this idea of who we are and want to ensure that it stays intact. When something happens that challenges that idea, it can be tough to handle. That's why we might get defensive or upset when someone says something negative about us or our work.

As a teenager, it's common to feel like you're not good enough or that you don't measure up to others. These feelings can be tough to shake, but self-affirmations can be a powerful tool in your arsenal. By focusing on your positive qualities and reminding yourself of your worth, you can boost your self-esteem and quiet that negative self-talk.

But self-affirmations aren't just feel-good mantras - there's actual science behind why they work. According to research, practicing self-affirmations regularly can have a range of benefits, including improved academic performance, better decision-making, and better physical health (Cohen & Sherman, 2014). So, whether you're trying to ace a test, make a new friend, or overcome a personal challenge, self-affirmations can help you get there.

Are you ready to learn more about the science behind self-affirmations and how they can benefit you as a teenager? Let's dive in!

Self-affirmations can help you build a positive mindset and set you up for success in all areas of your life. By focusing on the positive and reminding yourself of your worth and potential, you can approach challenges with a sense of confidence and optimism. This can help you achieve your goals, build strong relationships, and create a truly fulfilling life.

In this chapter, we'll dive into the research on self-affirmation theory and explore how it works. We'll look at the different ways that self-affirmations can be used, from boosting academic performance to improving relationships with others. We'll also take a closer look at the brain and how it responds to self-affirmations and explore the psychological mechanisms behind this fascinating phenomenon.

So if you're ready to learn more about how self-affirmations can help you overcome challenges and achieve your goals, let's dive in and discover the science behind self-affirmations together!

What is Self-Affirmation Theory?

Have you ever heard of the self-affirmation theory? It's a fascinating topic in psychology that explores how people protect their sense of self when faced with threats or challenges.

Self-affirmation theory suggests that people desire to maintain a positive view of themselves. Events that challenge this view can cause stress and lead to defensive responses. This can hamper performance and growth, which is obviously not ideal.

However, researchers have found that self-affirmation can help curb these adverse outcomes. Self-affirmations work when people write about their core personal values. These interventions focus on an in-depth view of oneself, weakening the effects of threats on personal integrity.

Self-affirmations have been shown to improve education, health, and relationship outcomes, with benefits that can persist for months and years. It's a powerful tool that we can use to maintain our sense of self and thrive in the face of challenges.

Self-affirmations can include doing activities that affirm the self, writing down core-personal values, and repeating those values. Self-affirmations given at these times can help people navigate difficulties and set them on a better path. Their confidence in their ability to overcome future challenges may grow and thus assist in coping and resilience for the next adversity in a self-reinforcing narrative (Cohen et al., 2009).

Why is it Important to Understand Self-Affirmation?

Do you ever feel like you're not good enough or that you don't measure up to the expectations of your friends? Or maybe you've experienced a setback or failure that made you doubt your abilities among your peers. If you've ever felt this way, then understanding the concept of self-affirmation could be helpful for you.

Self-affirmation theory is about how we protect and maintain our self-worth and integrity. It explains why we often react defensively to criticism or failure and why this can sometimes hold us back from reaching our full potential. By understanding self-affirmation, we can learn strategies to boost our self-esteem and overcome these adverse reactions.

So, why is it important to understand self-affirmation as a teenager? Well, for one thing, it can help you better understand yourself and why you react the way you do in certain situations. It can also provide you with tools to cope with challenges and setbacks more positively, improving your mental health and well-being. Self-affirmation can positively impact many areas of your life, including your relationships, academic and career success, and overall happiness.

In short, understanding self-affirmation can help you become more resilient, confident, and successful in life.

The Science Behind Self-Affirmations: How They Affect The Brain And Behavior

This section will dive into the science behind self-affirmations and how they affect the brain and behavior.

As I said earlier, self-affirmations are positive statements that you speak to yourself to boost your confidence and self-esteem. They can be as simple as "I am capable" or "I am strong."

Now, let's discuss how self-affirmations affect your brain as a teenager.

When you repeat a self-affirmation to yourself, it activates the reward centers in your brain. This leads to the release of dopamine, a chemical that makes you feel good.

But it's not just about feeling good in the moment. Repeatedly saying positive statements to yourself can actually change the way your brain works in the long term. It can strengthen neural pathways related to self-worth and positivity while weakening pathways related to negative self-talk.

You know that feeling when you try something new, and it turns out you're good at it? Or when you have a bad day, and it feels like nothing is going right? Those experiences can affect how we see ourselves and our self-worth.

But the thing is, the self-system is pretty flexible. That means that we can change how we see ourselves based on our experiences and how we interpret them. So even if we have a terrible day, we don't have to let it define us.

Think about it - have you ever had a time when you didn't think you were good at something, but then you practiced and got better? Or maybe you used to see yourself a certain way, but then you had an experience that made you see things differently. That's all thanks to the flexibility of the self-system.

Of course, it's not always easy to change how we see ourselves. Sometimes we get stuck in patterns of negative thinking or self-doubt. But the good news is that we can work on changing those patterns too. We can practice positive self-talk, focus on our strengths, and surround ourselves with people who lift us up and support us.

So if you feel stuck in a certain mindset or thinking pattern, remember that you have the power to change it. Keep building a positive self-image, and don't be afraid to try new things and challenge yourself. Who knows, you might surprise yourself with what you're capable of!

You know when someone criticizes you or something you've worked hard on, and you feel you must defend yourself? That's a pretty typical response, and it comes from our motivation to protect how we see ourselves.

See, we all have this idea of who we are and what we're worth. It can be tough to handle when someone says something that challenges that idea. Our first instinct might be to get defensive or lash out at another person.

But the thing is, defensive responses aren't always the best way to handle things. They can make the other person feel like you're not listening to them and make you feel worse in the long run. Plus, they don't solve anything.

So, how does this translate into behavior? When you have a stronger sense of self-worth and positivity, you're more likely to take on challenges and pursue your goals. You're also more likely to cope better with stress and setbacks.

What are Self-Affirmations, and How Can They Benefit Teenagers?

Let's start by talking about what self-affirmations are. Simply put, self-affirmations are positive statements you make about who you are, what you're capable of, and what you value. These statements are designed to counteract negative self-talk and build your confidence and self-esteem.

It is an act that demonstrates one's adequacy of self. Many events in a given day are seen as relevant to the self in some way, enabling people. Affirmations are small inputs into the self-system that can have a significant effect because a healthy self-system is motivated to maintain the integrity and generate affirming meanings.

Now, you might be thinking, "Okay, that sounds nice, but do they work?" The answer is yes! Studies have shown that self-affirmations can have a real impact on how we think and behave. When you repeat positive statements to yourself, you start to internalize them and believe them on a deeper level. This can help you feel more confident, capable, and resilient, even in the face of challenges.

So, how can self-affirmations benefit you as a teenager? For one, they can help you overcome negative self-talk and the pressure to conform to others' expectations. By reminding yourself of your unique strengths and values, you can feel more comfortable being yourself and pursuing your own goals and interests. Self-affirmations can also help you manage stress and anxiety, which are common challenges for teenagers.

Three Key Things to Know About Self-Affirmations

1. With time people may commit themselves to a particular self-definition (student, son). However, the self can draw on various roles to maintain its integrity. The motive is to keep a global narrative of oneself and adapt ("I am a good person"), not a specific self-concept (e.g., "I am a good student")(Aronson, 1969).

2. The motive for self-integrity is not to be superior or excellent but to be "good enough" to be competent enough in domains to feel that one is a good person, moral and adaptive.

3. The motive for self-integrity is not to praise oneself but rather to act in ways worthy of esteem or praise.

The Psychology of Self-Integrity

Self-integrity refers to our perception of ourselves as individuals. We all have a sense of who we are and what we stand for. This sense of self is important because it shapes our thoughts, emotions, and behaviors. When we encounter situations or events that threaten our sense of self, we may experience stress or anxiety. This is where the concept of self-defense comes into play.

Self-defense refers to how we protect our sense of self. We do this by using self-affirmation - reminding ourselves of our core values and beliefs. Doing so reinforces our sense of self, which helps us cope with the challenges and stressors we encounter.

Self-affirmation can take many forms, but by focusing on the positive aspects of our lives, we can help maintain our self-integrity, which can lead to better mental health and well-being.

Teenagers need to understand the psychology of self-integrity and self-defense because it can help them develop resilience and cope with life's challenges.

Why Do We Need to Protect Our Self-Integrity as a Teenager

Have you ever felt like someone has insulted or criticized you, and it ruined your day? Or maybe you felt not good enough compared to someone else? Don't worry; it's normal to feel that way sometimes.

The truth is, as human beings, we all have a deep desire to protect our self-integrity. This means we want to maintain a positive view of ourselves and ensure our self-worth is not threatened. We want to feel like we're good people worthy of love, respect, and success.

When our self-integrity is threatened, it can cause us to feel stressed, anxious, or even angry. That's because our brains are wired to respond to perceived threats to protect ourselves. And if we don't preserve our self-integrity, it can negatively impact our mental health and well-being.

So, why do we need to protect our self-integrity? Well, because it's essential for our personal growth, relationships, and success in life. Feeling good about ourselves makes us more likely to take on new challenges and pursue our goals. We're also more likely to have positive relationships with others because we feel secure in ourselves.

However, protecting our self-integrity doesn't mean we must always be perfect or never make mistakes. It's essential to recognize that we're all human and imperfect. What's important is that we learn to accept ourselves, flaws and all, and focus on our strengths and positive qualities.

How Can Self-Affirmation Help Maintain Self-Integrity?

Hey there, teenager! Have you heard that self-affirmation can help you maintain your self-integrity? Let's dive into it!

As I said early, self-affirmation is a technique that involves reflecting on your core values and beliefs and writing about them. It may sound simple, but it can significantly impact your well-being and success. According to Sherman and Cohen (2006), here are some ways that self-affirmation can help you maintain self-integrity as a teenager:

1. Boosts self-esteem: By affirming your core values, you remind yourself of your worth and what makes you unique. This can increase your self-esteem and confidence, making facing challenges easier and staying true to yourself.

2. Reduces stress: When you face a challenge or a threat to your self-integrity, it can cause stress and anxiety. Self-

affirmation can help reduce this stress by reminding you of your values and strengths.

3. Encourages growth: Self-affirmation can help you identify areas of growth and change. By reflecting on your values and beliefs, you can discover what is most important to you and work towards personal growth and development.

4. Improves relationships: When you are true to yourself and your values, you are more likely to attract positive relationships. Self-affirmation can help you identify and align your values with your relationships, leading to more fulfilling connections with others.

Remember, self-affirmation is not a one-time fix. It is a practice that must be consistently done to reap its benefits. So take some time to reflect on your values and beliefs and write them down. You might be surprised at the positive impact it can have on your life! Now that we know what self-affirmations are, how do they change the brain from thinking negatively to positively? The answer is neuroplasticity.

The Science of Neuroplasticity

Hey there, teenagers! Have you ever heard of the term "neuroplasticity"? It may sound like a complicated word, but it's pretty cool and important to understand.

In simple terms, neuroplasticity refers to the brain's ability to change and adapt throughout our lives in response to different experiences. This means that our brains are not fixed or rigid but are malleable and can be shaped by our actions and thoughts.

It was once thought that the brain could only develop during childhood, but now we know it can continue to grow and change throughout our lives. This means that even as teenagers, our brains constantly change and adapt to new situations and experiences.

So, why is this important to know? Well, understanding neuroplasticity means that we have the power to shape our own brains through our actions and experiences. We can intentionally work to strengthen specific parts of our brain, such as our memory or our ability to focus, by practicing and engaging in activities that challenge those areas.

On the other hand, if we repeatedly engage in harmful or unhealthy behaviors, our brains may become wired to continue those behavior patterns, which can negatively impact our mental and physical health.

But here's the good news: even if we have developed specific patterns of behavior or thought, we can still work to rewire our brains through intentional practices like self-affirmation, meditation, and therapy.

In short, the science of neuroplasticity shows us that our brains are constantly changing and adapting, and we can shape our brains through our actions and experiences.

Now that we've discussed the science behind self-affirmations and how they can benefit you, let's dive into how you can start incorporating and creating effective self-affirmations that work for you into your daily routine. By customizing your self-affirmations to your personal needs and goals, you can create a powerful tool for improving your mindset and achieving your dreams. So, let's get started!

CHAPTER THREE

BEST PRACTICES FOR SELF-AFFIRMATION

Welcome back, friends!

In the last chapter, we discussed the science behind self-affirmation and its impact on the brain. Now, let's take it a step further and dive into some of the best practices for self-affirmation.

We'll explore the power of positive self-talk and how it can help you shift your mindset and approach challenges more confidently and optimistically. We'll also talk about the importance of self-care and how taking care of yourself can boost your self-esteem and sense of worth.

But that's not all! We'll also cover the importance of setting goals and celebrating your achievements, whether big or small. By acknowledging and celebrating your successes, you'll start to see just how incredible you are.

So get ready to learn some great new strategies for building up your self-esteem and taking control of your life. Remember, you are capable of great things, and with the power of self-affirmation, nothing can stand in your way!

How to Create Effective Self-Affirmations That Work For You

You have heard of self-affirmation throughout the last chapter. It's a fancy way of saying that it's important to remind yourself of all the awesome things you're capable of. And guess what? Psychologists and researchers have found that doing this can seriously benefit your mental health, like helping you deal with stress. Here's the catch: it's not just about saying a bunch of nice things to yourself in the mirror. Effective self-affirmation is all about figuring out what you value and using that as a foundation for your affirmations. That's why in this book, I'll give you some affirmations to use and help you personalize them so that they speak to what's important to you.

So why is self-affirmation so important? We all want to see ourselves as good and competent people, right? But sometimes, life throws us curveballs, and we start to doubt ourselves. Maybe you fail a test, get criticized, or perhaps social media makes you feel like you're not measuring up. That's where self-affirmation comes in - it's like a shield that protects you from those negative thoughts and helps you maintain a positive self-image.

By focusing on what you value and reminding yourself of all the awesome things you've accomplished, you can boost your self-esteem and improve your ability to cope with whatever life throws. So let's get started on this journey of self-affirmation and discover just how amazing you really are!

We've talked about the importance of self-affirmation, and now let's dive into how you can make your affirmations even more effective.

According to some self-help experts, there are a few key steps you can take to try self-affirmations (Wong, 2018).

First up, it's all about developing a multidimensional life. This means getting involved in multiple things that contribute to your identity, like your passions, school, and relationships with family and friends. You have more to affirm about yourself when you have a well-rounded life!

Next, you want to make sure your affirmations are authentic. What does that mean? Your affirmations should be consistent with your values and beliefs about yourself. So take some time to think about what matters to you and what you want to affirm.

Finally, building a daily habit around your affirmation is vital. It's not just about thinking or saying your affirmation but also behaving in ways that are consistent with your beliefs. That means taking action to support your affirmation and make it a reality.

So there you have it - three ways to make your affirmations even more effective. Remember, self-affirmation is about boosting your confidence and reminding yourself of all the awesome things you're capable of.

Creating effective self-affirmations is a great place to start if you want to improve your mindset and boost your confidence. But how do you go about creating affirmations that work for you? So, let's dive in! In this section, we'll explore some tips and strategies for crafting powerful self-affirmations that resonate with you and help you achieve your goals. Whether you're struggling with self-doubt or anxiety or just need a daily dose of positivity, these tips will help you create affirmations that genuinely work for you.

Here are some tips and strategies to help you get started:

1. Start with your goals: Identifying what exactly you want to achieve or improve is essential. Do you want to improve your grades in school? Make more meaningful connections with friends? Boost your self-confidence? Whatever it is, once you have a clear goal in mind, you can start crafting affirmations that are specific to your needs.

By repeating this statement to yourself regularly, you can start to believe it more deeply and feel more motivated to work towards your goals.

When crafting affirmations, make them specific, positive, and present tense. Instead of saying, "I will be more confident in the future," say, "I am confident and capable right now." This helps to reinforce the idea that you already possess the qualities you want to cultivate. Additionally, try to make your affirmations as personal and meaningful as possible. They should resonate with you on a deep level and feel like they're in alignment with your actual values and desires.

So, to sum it up: identify your goals, craft specific and positive affirmations that align with them, and repeat them to yourself regularly. With some practice and persistence, you'll be well on your way to achieving your goals and improving your life!

2. Keep it positive: When creating affirmations, framing them positively and in the present tense is crucial. This means

focusing on what you want to achieve or cultivate rather than what you want to avoid or eliminate.

For example, let's say you have an upcoming test and feel nervous. Instead of saying, "I won't fail my test," which emphasizes failure, try saying, "I am capable and prepared for my test." This affirmation emphasizes your confidence and ability to do well, which can help you feel more empowered and motivated.

When affirmations are framed positively, they can help shift your mindset towards a more optimistic and solution-focused perspective. Rather than dwelling on what could go wrong, you're focusing on what you can do to create a positive outcome. This can help to reduce anxiety, build confidence, and improve overall well-being.

So, next time you craft affirmations, remember to keep them positive and present tense. Doing so creates a powerful tool to help you achieve your goals and cultivate a more positive mindset.

3. Be specific: Another vital aspect to consider when creating affirmations is to be as detailed as possible. The more specific you can make your affirmations, the more effective they'll be in helping you achieve your goals.

For example, let's say you want to improve your math skills. Instead of saying, "I am good at math," which is a general statement, try saying, "I understand and excel at algebra." This affirmation is more specific and targeted, which can help to reinforce your confidence and ability in that particular area.

When affirmations are specific, they give your brain a clear and tangible target to focus on. This can help to create a stronger connection between your beliefs and actions and increase your motivation to work towards your goals. In contrast, general or vague affirmations may not have as much impact because they don't provide a clear direction for your thoughts and actions.

So, when creating your affirmations, try to be as specific as possible. Think about the area or skill you want to improve and craft a statement that directly addresses that goal. Doing so will create a powerful tool to help you achieve your aspirations and build a more positive mindset.

4. Use personal language: Use language that resonates with your own experiences and emotions so that your affirmations can impact your mindset and behavior.

For example, let's say you want to improve your self-worth. Instead of saying, "People like me," which might feel generic and disconnected from your personal experiences, try saying, "I am loved and valued by those around me." This more personal and specific affirmation speaks directly to your emotions and experiences.

When affirmations feel personal, they can help create a deeper connection between your beliefs and your sense of self. This can increase your motivation to work towards your goals and reinforce positive behaviors and habits. On the other hand, if your affirmations feel disconnected or generic, they may not impact your mindset or behavior as much.

So, when creating your affirmations, try to use language that feels personal and meaningful to you. Think about your own experiences and emotions, and craft a statement that speaks directly to your own values and aspirations.

5. Repeat, repeat, repeat: Repeating your affirmations is key to making them a part of your subconscious mindset and creating lasting change.

The more you repeat your affirmations, the more they'll sink in and become ingrained in your beliefs and behaviors. So, try saying them out loud every day, or write them down in a journal. You can also try incorporating them into your meditation or visualization practices.

Repeating your affirmations regularly can help to reinforce positive beliefs and behaviors and create a more optimistic and empowered mindset. It can also help to counteract negative self-talk and reinforce positive self-talk, which can be a powerful tool in improving your mental health and well-being.

However, it's important to remember that repetition alone is not enough. You also need to take action towards your goals and make positive changes in your life. Affirmations can help reinforce positive beliefs and behaviors but cannot replace concrete action and effort.

So, when using affirmations, repeat them regularly and make them a part of your daily routine.

6. Believe in yourself: Ultimately, the power of affirmations comes from the belief and trust that they'll help you achieve your goals.

When you say your affirmations, please focus on the positive feelings and emotions they evoke. The more you believe in your affirmations, the more they'll resonate with your subconscious mind and help create positive change in your life. Try to visualize yourself achieving your goals and feeling proud and accomplished.

It's also important to remember that believing in yourself is key to achieving success in any area of your life. When you trust your abilities and believe in your potential, you're more likely to take risks, try new things, and overcome obstacles.

Creating effective self-affirmations takes practice, but it's a powerful tool for improving your mindset and achieving your dreams. So, give it a try and see how it works for you!

Using Self-Affirmations to Overcome Self-Doubt And Build Self-Esteem

If you ever find yourself struggling with self-doubt or low self-esteem. It's totally normal - we all have moments when we feel unsure of ourselves. But the good news is that self-affirmations can be a powerful tool for overcoming these negative feelings and building self-confidence while growing up. Here are some tips for using self-affirmations to boost your self-esteem:

1. Identify your negative thoughts: Let's talk about how to identify and transform negative thoughts into positive affirmations. It all starts by becoming aware of your negative thoughts or beliefs about yourself.

So, take some time to reflect on your thoughts and beliefs. Do you often tell yourself that you're not good enough? That you'll never succeed? Write these thoughts down, and then flip them around into positive affirmations.

For example, if you think, "I'm not good enough," try flipping it around into "I am capable and worthy." If you often tell yourself, "I'll never succeed," try affirming, "I can achieve my goals and dreams."

By flipping your negative thoughts around into positive affirmations, you're reprogramming your mind to focus on positive beliefs and self-talk. This can help counteract negative thought patterns and improve your overall self-worth and confidence.

And remember, the power of positive self-talk and affirmations can be a powerful tool in improving your mental health and well-being.

2. Focus on your strengths: When crafting affirmations, focus on your strengths and accomplishments. One powerful way to do this is by reminding yourself of times when you've succeeded and the qualities that helped you do so.

So, take some time to reflect on your past successes and accomplishments. Think about the qualities and strengths that helped you achieve those successes. Maybe you're a great communicator or have a problem-solving talent. Whatever your strengths are, try to focus on them when crafting your affirmations.

For example, instead of saying, "I'm not good enough," try saying, "I am capable and accomplished." By focusing on your strengths and past successes, you're reminding yourself of the qualities that make you capable and worthy.

By focusing on your strengths, you're reinforcing positive beliefs and self-talk.

3. Be kind to yourself: As a teenager, it's common to experience a lot of pressure and self-doubt, but it's important to remember to treat yourself with kindness and compassion.

When crafting affirmations, use language that is gentle and supportive. Instead of being critical or harsh on yourself, try to be your biggest cheerleader. Use affirmations like "I am worthy of love and respect" or "I am confident in my abilities and strengths."

Remember that you are still growing and learning, and making mistakes along the way is okay. Treat yourself with the same kindness and understanding you would offer to a friend going through a tough time.

By using gentle and supportive affirmations, you can shift your mindset towards more positive self-talk and beliefs. This can have a significant impact on your overall well-being and self-esteem.

4. Use visualization: Another great tool to use when crafting affirmations is visualization. Visualizing yourself succeeding and feeling confident can help reinforce positive beliefs and make them feel more natural.

Next time you're saying your affirmations, try to imagine yourself achieving your goals. Visualize acing that test, making new friends, or succeeding in whatever you want to accomplish. Use all your senses to create a vivid picture in your mind - what does it look like? Sound like? Feel like?

By visualizing yourself succeeding, you can start to build up your confidence and reinforce positive beliefs about yourself.

This can help you stay motivated and focused as you work towards your goals.

Remember also to be kind to yourself and recognize that success looks different for everyone. Don't compare yourself to others, and celebrate your own unique accomplishments along the way.

5. Repeat, repeat, repeat: Hey, teenager, here's a reminder that repetition is critical when it comes to self-affirmation practice. Whether you're saying your affirmations out loud every day or writing them down in a journal, the more you repeat them, the more they'll become ingrained in your subconscious mind.

Remember, teenagers, using self-affirmations to overcome self-doubt and build self-esteem takes time and practice. Don't get discouraged if you don't see results right away. The key is to stick with it and be consistent. Try incorporating self-affirmations into your daily routine, whether saying them in the morning or writing them down before bed. You might even find it helpful to set reminders on your phone to say your affirmations throughout the day.

And don't forget, self-affirmations should be that one tool in your toolbox for building confidence and overcoming negative self-talk.

Incorporating Self-Affirmations Into Your Daily Routine For Maximum Impact

How do you incorporate self-affirmations into your daily routine? It's easy! Start by choosing a few positive statements that resonate with you. Some examples might include "I am capable of achieving my goals" or "I am worthy of love and respect." Write these statements down and keep them in a place where you'll see them every day, like in your mirror or in your planner.

Next, set aside a few minutes each day to repeat these affirmations to yourself. You can do this in the morning when you wake up, before bed, or anytime throughout the day when you need a little boost. It's important to say these affirmations out loud and with conviction, really believing in the positive message you're giving yourself.

Over time, incorporating self-affirmations into your daily routine can have a powerful impact on your overall mindset and outlook on life. You'll start to see yourself more positively and have more confidence in your abilities. So give it a try! Choose a few self-affirmations that resonate with you and start repeating them to yourself every day. You might be surprised at how much of a difference it can make!

Overcoming Common Barriers to Using Self-Affirmations And How to Stay Motivated

One common obstacle is feeling self-conscious or embarrassed about saying positive things to yourself. It can feel silly initially, but try practicing in private or with a trusted friend until you feel more comfortable saying them out loud.

Another obstacle is feeling like you don't have enough time in the day to do it. But incorporating self-affirmations into your daily routine doesn't have to take a lot of time. Even just a few minutes a day can make a big difference. You can say your affirmations while brushing your teeth, during your commute, or before bed.

Staying motivated can also be challenging, especially if you don't see results immediately. Remember that building self-esteem and confidence takes time and consistency. Sticking with it is crucial even when you don't feel it's working. You can also try adding variety to your affirmations, switching them up every few weeks to keep things fresh and exciting.

Another helpful tip is to track your progress. Please write down your affirmations and the date, and keep track of how you feel before and after saying them. You might be surprised at how much your mindset and outlook can change over time.

So don't give up, teenager! Overcoming common obstacles to using self-affirmations takes time and effort, but the results are well worth it. Remember that you are worthy of love and respect and that positive self-talk can be a powerful tool for building self-esteem and confidence. Keep at it; before you know it, you'll see the positive impact on your life.

Remember, self-affirmations can be a powerful tool for building confidence and self-esteem, but they are just one piece of the puzzle. It's also important to practice self-care, set realistic goals, and surround yourself with positive influences to truly thrive as a teenager, and you will surely achieve a whole lot in the shortest time.

Hey teenagers! Let's take a journey together and discover how to declare our affirmations. Join me in the next chapter, and I'll guide you through the process step by step.

CHAPTER FOUR

AFFIRMATIONS ON SELF-CONCEPT

I respect and accept myself.

Feeling confident is not always easy, especially when the world can be challenging. But remember that you're unique and special in your own way, and you deserve to treat yourself with kindness and compassion.

Personalize it: Looking back on your past, what were some of the things you did or thought that made it hard for you to feel good about yourself? Let's reflect together!

_____

_____

_____

_____

_____

_____

_____

Put it into practice: For each moment you can recall, Take a moment to forgive yourself and appreciate who you are.

I am proud to be Black.

Embrace your heritage, culture, and unique experiences, and know that they all make you the exceptional individual you are. Remember that your skin color is a beautiful part of you, and don't let anyone tell you otherwise.

Personalize it: What were some of the factors that contributed to the feelings of not embracing your race, and how did you respond to those challenges? Please take a moment to reflect on moments when you may have felt like you failed to embrace your Blackness and write them down entirely.

_____

_____

_____

_____

_____

_____

_____

_____

_____

Put it into practice: Find ways to celebrate your Blackness, whether through learning about your heritage, connecting with your community, or sharing your experiences with others.

I am designed for greatness.

Embrace your strengths and talents, and don't be afraid to take risks and pursue your passions. Remember that success is not defined by external achievements or accomplishments but by your own personal growth and progress.

Personalize it: Have you ever felt that you were destined for greatness but somehow stumbled along the way? Reflect on them and try jotting down a few moments when you didn't quite meet your expectations.

_____

_____

_____

_____

_____

_____

_____

_____

Put it into practice: Start by setting some goals for yourself and taking small daily steps toward achieving them. Remember, greatness is within reach!

I have a powerful voice.

Don't ever underestimate the power of your voice. You have the ability to make a difference. Speak up, express your thoughts and opinions, and make yourself heard.

Personalize it: Have you ever held back from expressing your thoughts and opinions? Take a moment and think about a time when you didn't speak up, even though you wanted to. What stopped you from admitting your powerful voice? Write down a few of those reasons.

_____

_____

_____

_____

_____

_____

_____

_____

_____

Put it into practice: Don't be afraid to speak up and use your voice to impact your community or the world positively.

I am a Leader

You can inspire and empower others with your words and actions. Don't let anyone tell you you're too young to be a leader because you have what it takes to be one. Keep being your unique self and leading by example because the world needs more leaders like you!

Personalize it: Think about when you stepped up as a leader. What are some qualities that make a good leader?

_____

_____

_____

_____

_____

_____

_____

_____

_____

_____

_____

Put it into practice: Don't be afraid to step up, take charge, and positively impact your community or the world.

I am smart.

Embrace your intelligence and use it to achieve your goals, pursue your passions, and positively impact the world.

Personalize it: What held you back from embracing your intelligence? Was it self-doubt, negative comments from others, or something else? Take a moment and write down why you may have struggled to recognize your intelligence.

_____

_____

_____

_____

_____

_____

_____

_____

_____

_____

_____

Put it into practice: Don't be afraid to challenge yourself, take on new tasks, and pursue your passions.

I have forgiven myself and have let go of my past mistakes.

Remember, we all make mistakes, and that's okay. What matters is how we learn and grow from them. It's not always easy to let go of past mistakes, but it's an important step toward healing and moving forward.

Personalize it: Consider a time when you may have held onto guilt, shame, or regret. What made it difficult for you to move forward and release those feelings? Take a moment and write down a few reasons you may have struggled to forgive yourself.

_____

_____

_____

_____

_____

_____

_____

_____

Put it into practice: If you haven't forgiven yourself for past mistakes, take the time and do so now. You deserve to live a happy and fulfilling life, free from the weight of past mistakes.

I only think thoughts that support the best version of me.

Remember, our thoughts have a powerful impact on our lives, so it's important to be mindful of them. Whenever you catch yourself thinking negatively or putting yourself down, take a deep breath and ask yourself if that thought is helping you become the best version of yourself.

Personalize it: Have you ever caught yourself thinking negative thoughts that don't support the best version of you? Please take a moment to reflect on any negative self-talk you've had recently, and write it down.

_____

_____

_____

_____

_____

_____

_____

_____

_____

Put it into practice: Turn those negative thoughts from above into positive ones. Changing our thought patterns takes an approach, but it's worth it. You've got this!

I am so strong that nothing can disturb my peace of mind.

Keep focusing on your inner strength and resilience. Believe in yourself and your ability to overcome any challenge. And remember, peace of mind is within your control. Even amid chaos, you can choose to stay calm and centered.

Personalize it: Have you ever experienced a situation where you felt like you were losing your peace of mind, despite believing that you are strong enough to handle anything that comes your way? Think about what triggered those feelings and how you reacted. Then, write them down.

_____

_____

_____

_____

_____

_____

_____

_____

Put it into practice: Focus on positive self-talk, take deep breaths and visualize yourself staying calm and centered in the face of adversity.

I think well of myself and only speak kindly to myself.

It's important to remember that how we talk to ourselves can significantly impact our overall well-being and confidence. By speaking kindly to yourself, you're showing yourself love and respect, and that's something to be proud of.

Personalize it: have you ever failed to think well of yourself and only speak kindly to yourself? Maybe you had a bad day and let your negative thoughts take over. Take time to reflect and write down instances when you didn't speak kindly to yourself.

_____

_____

_____

_____

_____

_____

_____

_____

_____

Put it into practice: Whenever you think or say something negative about yourself, I want you to stop and rephrase it positively and kindly.

My optimism for life shines through in
everything I think, say, and do.

Optimism is a powerful force that can help you overcome challenges and achieve your goals. When you approach life with a positive attitude, you're more likely to see opportunities instead of obstacles, and you'll be better equipped to handle whatever comes your way.

Personalize it: Take a moment and reflect on times when you've failed to let your optimism shine through. I want you to take a moment and write down any instances when you didn't let your optimism shine through.

_____

_____

_____

_____

_____

_____

_____

_____

Put it into practice: Spend time with people who uplift and inspire you, and seek out activities that bring you joy and fulfillment.

I am confident in myself and my abilities.

When you believe in yourself and your abilities, you're more likely to take risks, try new things, and push yourself to be the best you can be. Confidence isn't something you're born with - it's something you can cultivate over time.

Personalize it: Have there been times when you didn't feel confident in yourself or your abilities? Maybe you didn't speak up in class even though you knew the answer. Whatever the case may be, please think about what held you back and write it down.

_____

_____

_____

_____

_____

_____

_____

_____

_____

Put it into practice: Try to set achievable goals for yourself and work towards them; with that, you're building your confidence and proving to yourself that you're capable of success. Write down your goals for this week and stick to them.

Every day in every way, I am getting better and better.

Remember that personal growth and improvement are lifelong journeys. It's not about being perfect but rather about striving to be the best version of yourself that you can be.

Personalize it: I want you to take a moment and reflect on those moments. What specifically made you feel like you weren't getting better? Was it a setback or a mistake you made? Did you feel like you weren't making progress toward your goals? Write down those moments and reflect on them.

_____

_____

_____

_____

_____

_____

_____

_____

_____

Put it into practice: Focus on making minor improvements every day. Break down your goals into smaller, manageable steps and work on them consistently.

I am resilient, and I can't be destroyed.

Whatever life throws your way, you have the strength and courage to face it head-on and overcome any obstacle. It's okay to stumble and fall sometimes; that's a part of life. But remember, you're becoming stronger and more resilient every time you get back up.

Personalize it: Can you think of a time when you felt like you weren't resilient enough? Maybe you faced a difficult situation and didn't know how to handle it, or perhaps you felt like giving up instead of pushing through. Take some time to write down those moments.

_____

_____

_____

_____

_____

_____

_____

_____

_____

Put it into practice: Don't hesitate to ask for help. Surround yourself with supportive people who will lift you up when you're feeling down.

I am brave; fear does not exist within me.

When you're feeling afraid, take a moment to breathe deeply and remind yourself of your strength. Remember, you are capable of amazing things! Believe in yourself and your ability to overcome any challenge that comes your way.

Personalize it: Have you ever felt like you weren't brave enough? Maybe you were afraid to speak up in class, try a new sport, or ask someone out on a date. I encourage you to take a moment and write down any situations where you felt like you failed to live up to your affirmation.

_____

_____

_____

_____

_____

_____

_____

Put it into practice: Don't hesitate to step out of your comfort zone and try new things. Whether it's joining a new club or sport or simply speaking up in class, take small steps towards being brave every day.

I have been given endless talents, which I will utilize today.

You are a unique and special individual with many talents and abilities that make you shine. Whether you're a fantastic artist, a talented athlete, or a gifted musician, it's time to utilize those talents to the fullest.

Personalize it: Have you ever felt you failed to utilize your talents? Perhaps you didn't pursue a hobby or skill you were interested in because you felt like you weren't good enough. It's time to face those feelings and write them down.

_____

_____

_____

_____

_____

_____

_____

_____

Put it into practice: Start by identifying your talents and interests. What are you passionate about? What makes you happy? Once you have a list of your abilities, consider how to incorporate them into your daily life.

My confidence isn't built off compliments,
but it's built on competence.

It's important to remember that confidence comes from within. While compliments can certainly feel good, true belief comes from knowing that you have the skills and abilities to handle any situation that comes your way.

Personalize it: Have you ever relied on compliments or sought external validation to feel confident? And have you ever had your confidence shaken when someone didn't give you the praise or recognition you were hoping for? Now, write those instances down.

_____

_____

_____

_____

_____

_____

_____

_____

Put it into practice: Pick one skill or activity you've wanted to learn or improve on and commit to practicing it every day for the next week.

I always stay calm under pressure.

There are concrete steps we can take to stay calm under pressure. One effective technique is deep breathing. When you feel yourself getting stressed or anxious, please take a moment to breathe in deeply, hold it for a few seconds, and then release it slowly. This can help regulate your heart rate and calm your mind.

Personalize it: I encourage you to take a moment and think about times when you've struggled to stay calm. What were the circumstances? How did you react? Write down your thoughts and reflections.

_____

_____

_____

_____

_____

_____

_____

_____

Put it into practice: The next time you find yourself in a high-pressure situation, take a deep breath and remind yourself of your inner strength and ability to stay calm. Remember that you have faced challenges before and come out on top, and you can do it again.

I am a warrior.

Remember that strength and courage come in many forms. It could mean standing up for yourself or others, facing a difficult challenge, or simply getting through a tough day. Always know that you have the inner strength and resilience to handle it.

Personalize it: Think about a situation where you didn't feel as strong or courageous as you would have liked. Maybe it was a challenging conversation, a difficult test, or even just trying something new. Ask yourself: what held you back from feeling strong and courageous at that moment? Take some time to write down these challenges.

Put it into practice: Believe in yourself and your abilities, take risks, and never give up. You got this!

I am a responsible person.

Being responsible is a characteristic that will take you far in life. It shows that you are dependable and trustworthy; people will appreciate that. Remember that being responsible doesn't mean you can't have fun or make mistakes; it just means you're accountable for your actions and their consequences.

Personalize it: Can you think of a time when you didn't act responsibly? What were the consequences of your actions? Take some time to reflect on what you could have done differently and write them down.

_____

_____

_____

_____

_____

_____

_____

_____

_____

Put it into practice: List tasks or responsibilities you must complete. Then, prioritize them and create a schedule or to-do list to help you stay on track.

I am kind.

Remember, kindness is always a superpower! Being kind doesn't just benefit others; it also makes you feel good about yourself. Keep up the excellent work, and never underestimate the power of a simple act of kindness.

Personalize it: Have you ever felt you could have been kinder to someone? Maybe you missed an opportunity to show kindness or were unkind in a moment of frustration. Take a moment to reflect and write down any situations where you could have been kinder.

_____

_____

_____

_____

_____

_____

_____

_____

_____

_____

Put it into practice: Remember, making mistakes and learning from them is okay. Focus on being kinder moving forward!

I am creative.

Being creative is not about being perfect or having all the answers. It's about taking risks, trying new things, and expressing yourself uniquely. So go ahead, embrace your creativity, and let it shine!

Personalize it: In what ways do you feel creative? Take a moment to write them down creative activities or hobbies you enjoy.

_____

_____

_____

_____

_____

_____

_____

_____

_____

Put it into practice: Don't be afraid to experiment and try new things. Allow yourself to make mistakes and learn from them. And most importantly, have fun and enjoy the process! I challenge you to do something creative today.

I am an important and valuable person.

Your unique qualities and experiences make you one-of-a-kind, which is something to be proud of. You have the power to impact the world around you in positive ways and never let anyone make you feel otherwise. Keep being you and shining your light!

Personalize it: Do you often struggle with feeling like you're not important or valuable? Maybe you've had experiences where you didn't feel like your opinions or ideas mattered. Take a moment to reflect on those times and write them down.

_____

_____

_____

_____

_____

_____

_____

_____

_____

Put it into practice: Take more time to treat yourself with kindness and respect, set healthy boundaries, and pursue your passions and interests.

I will always help others.

Helping others not only benefits them, but it also brings happiness and fulfillment to your own life. When you offer a helping hand, you show empathy and compassion, which is truly beautiful.

Personalize it: Let's be honest, we all make mistakes sometimes, and that's okay! So, have there been any times when you've failed to help someone, even though you wanted to? Take a moment to think about it and jot down those instances when you didn't lend a helping hand, even though you could have.

_____

_____

_____

_____

_____

_____

_____

_____

_____

_____

_____

Put it into practice: I challenge you to find ways to help others today. Always make a conscious effort to offer assistance and be there for others.

I believe in myself, and I can do anything.

You can achieve amazing things, and it all starts with believing in yourself. When you have confidence in your abilities, you can overcome any obstacles that come your way.

Personalize it: Have there been times when you've failed to live up to this affirmation? Take a moment to think about the times when you didn't believe in yourself or doubted your abilities. Write them down and think about how you can approach similar situations differently in the future.

_____

_____

_____

_____

_____

_____

_____

_____

_____

_____

Put it into practice: Celebrate your accomplishments, no matter how small they may seem. This will boost your confidence and give you the motivation to keep going.

I am an intelligent being. My knowledge will grow.

Learning is a lifelong journey, and making mistakes along the way is okay. In fact, making mistakes is a natural part of the learning process. Embrace them, learn from them, and use them to grow and improve.

Personalize it: We all have moments when we doubt ourselves but recognize and learn from them. So, think back to when you felt like you weren't smart enough or capable enough. I want you to write down what you learned from that experience.

_____

_____

_____

_____

_____

_____

_____

_____

_____

_____

Put it into practice: Don't be afraid to tackle complex tasks and step out of your comfort zone. Challenges are opportunities to learn and grow this week.

I understand that my actions become habits,
so I will try and do the right thing.

Remember, no one is perfect, and we all make mistakes. But it's important to learn from those mistakes and try to improve.

Personalize it: Try to recall times when you regretted a choice. Maybe it was something small, like skipping homework, or something bigger, like lying to a friend. Write down what you learned from that experience. Did you realize that your choices have consequences? Write down your insights and use them to grow and improve.

_____

_____

_____

_____

_____

_____

_____

_____

Put it into practice: Surround yourself with people who hold you accountable and support your goals. Share your progress with them and celebrate your successes together.

I dare to try new things.

Trying new things can be scary and intimidating, but it can also be gratifying and exciting. When you step out of your comfort zone and try something new, you open yourself up to new experiences and opportunities.

Personalize it: Have you ever had a moment when you wanted to try something new but held yourself back? Think back to that moment and write them down.

_____

_____

_____

_____

_____

_____

_____

_____

_____

_____

Put it into practice: Trying new things doesn't have to be a vast, scary endeavor. Start small and gradually work your way up to more significant challenges.

I am going to be productive today.

It can be easy to get caught up in procrastination or distractions, but setting a goal to be productive can help you stay focused and motivated.

Personalize it: Have you ever had a day where you wanted to be productive but felt like you didn't get anything done? Take a moment to reflect on those times and think about what might have prevented you from being productive. Please write down your thoughts and use them as a learning opportunity to help you be more productive in the future.

_____

_____

_____

_____

_____

_____

_____

_____

_____

_____

Put it into practice: Make a to-do list or schedule for the day to help you stay organized and focused.

I deserve respect.

Remember that you deserve respect simply because you are a human being. You are valuable and worthy of being treated with kindness and dignity. If you ever find yourself feeling disrespected, it's okay to speak up and let others know how you feel. Remember to use "I" statements and be assertive but not aggressive.

Personalize it: Can you think of a time when you felt disrespected or undervalued? What happened, and how did you react? Kindly write them down.

_____

_____

_____

_____

_____

_____

_____

_____

_____

_____

Put it into practice: Surround yourself with positive people. Spend time with people who value and respect you for who you are.

I deserve good things.

Life can be tricky sometimes, and we may not always get what we want. And remember, deserving good things doesn't mean you have to be perfect or have everything figured out. It simply means that you recognize your own worth and value and are willing to work towards a life that makes you happy and fulfilled.

Personalize it: Can you think of a time when you didn't believe you deserved something good? What was holding you back? Please write it down, and let's work on replacing those negative thoughts with positive ones.

_____

_____

_____

_____

_____

_____

_____

_____

_____

_____

Put it into practice: When we believe we deserve good things, it becomes easier to attract positivity into our lives.

I am worthy of love and respect.

Dear teenager, you deserve love and respect simply for being you. You don't have to do anything special or be anyone else to earn it.

Personalize it: Can you share with me some instances where you didn't believe you deserved love and respect? Write it down, and let's work on replacing those negative thoughts with positive ones.

_____

_____

_____

_____

_____

_____

_____

_____

_____

_____

_____

Put it into practice: Take time to speak kindly to yourself, care for your body, and set healthy boundaries with others. Make self-love and self-respect a habit!

External factors do not determine my self-worth.

It's easy to get caught up in the external factors that seem to determine our worth - grades, popularity, social status, and appearance. But the truth is, your worth comes from within. You are valuable and worthy just for being you, no matter what anyone else may say.

Personalize it: Have you ever felt like external factors determined your self-worth? Maybe it was your grades, social media likes, or what others think of you. Write them down, and let's work together to build a stronger sense of self-worth that comes from within.

_____

_____

_____

_____

_____

_____

_____

_____

Put it into practice: Today, try to remind yourself that your worth comes from within consciously.

I am capable of achieving my goals and dreams.

Believe in yourself, teenager! You have the power to achieve your dreams and goals, no matter how big or small they may seem. Anything is possible with hard work, determination, and belief in yourself.

Personalize it: Have you ever failed to believe in yourself and your abilities to achieve what you want? Please write it down, and let's work on replacing those negative thoughts.

_____

_____

_____

_____

_____

_____

_____

_____

_____

_____

_____

Put it into practice: Take small steps towards your goals, believe in your abilities, and don't give up when things get tough.

I am capable of achieving my goals and dreams.

Believe in yourself, teenager! You have the power to achieve your dreams and goals, no matter how big or small they may seem. Anything is possible with hard work, determination, and belief in yourself.

Personalize it: Write down your goals and dreams for this upcoming year and some longer-term goals; think five years from now.

Put it into practice: Set realistic goals for yourself and work towards them consistently. Please don't give up on your dreams, and don't be afraid to ask for help when needed.

I accept myself for who I am, my flaws and all.

Accepting yourself can be difficult, especially when we are bombarded with messages telling us we must be perfect. But the truth is, nobody is perfect - and that's okay! You are unique and special just the way you are, flaws and all.

Personalize it: Have there been times when you struggled to accept certain things about yourself? What were they, and how did you come to terms with them?

_____

_____

_____

_____

_____

_____

_____

_____

_____

Put it into practice: Practice self-care and self-love. Focus on your strengths instead of your weaknesses. Treat yourself with kindness and compassion.

I am confident in my abilities.

Trust in yourself, teenager! You have abilities and skills that are unique to you, and you should have confidence in yourself and your potential. Believe that you are capable of achieving great things, and you will.

Personalize it: Can you think of a time when you felt less confident? What happened, and how did you work through those feelings? Write it down.

_____

_____

_____

_____

_____

_____

_____

_____

_____

_____

_____

Put it into practice: Take on challenges and try new things. Believe in yourself and your abilities. Celebrate your achievements and learn from your mistakes.

I am strong and resilient.

Life can be tough, but you are tougher. You have the strength and resilience to overcome any challenge that comes your way. Remember that setbacks are not failures but opportunities to learn and grow.

Personalize it: Have you ever faced a situation that tested your resilience? What was it, and how did you bounce back from it? Write it down.

_____

_____

_____

_____

_____

_____

_____

_____

_____

_____

Put it into practice: Face challenges head-on, and don't give up easily. Take care of yourself physically, mentally, and emotionally. Surround yourself with positive people and seek support when you need it.

I deserve happiness and joy.

You deserve to be a happy teenager. Don't let anyone or anything make you feel otherwise. You are worthy of joy and happiness.

Personalize it: Can you recall when you struggled to believe you deserved those things? What happened, and how did you overcome those feelings? Please write it down.

_____

_____

_____

_____

_____

_____

_____

_____

_____

_____

_____

_____

_____

Put it into practice: Find joy in the little things and prioritize your happiness. Do things that make you happy and spend time with people who uplift you.

I am intelligent and capable of learning new things.

You are a curious and intelligent teenager who can learn and grow. Embrace your curiosity and strive to learn new things every day. Don't let anyone make you feel otherwise.

Personalize it: Have you ever faced a situation where you felt like you couldn't learn something? What was it, and how did you work through that frustration?

_____

_____

_____

_____

_____

_____

_____

_____

_____

_____

_____

Put it into practice: Embrace a growth mindset and be open to learning new things. Seek out opportunities to expand your knowledge and skills.

I trust myself to make the right decisions.

Trust your instincts, teenager. You know yourself better than anyone else, and you have the power to make the right decisions for yourself. Don't let anyone pressure you into doing something that doesn't feel right to you.

Personalize it: Have you ever made a decision that you regretted? What happened, and how did you learn from that experience? Write it down.

_____

_____

_____

_____

_____

_____

_____

_____

_____

Put it into practice: Listen to your intuition and trust your instincts. Make decisions based on your values and beliefs, and don't be afraid to ask for advice from trusted friends and family.

I am proud of who I am becoming.

Celebrate your growth and progress, teenager! You are constantly evolving and becoming the person you are meant to be. Be proud of yourself and all that you have accomplished so far.

Personalize it: Have you ever felt you weren't living up to your potential? What was going on, and how did you take steps to reach your goals? Write it down.

_____

_____

_____

_____

_____

_____

_____

_____

_____

_____

Put it into practice: Reflect on your personal growth and celebrate your achievements. Rather than comparing yourself to others, focus on your progress and how far you've come. Keep striving to become the best version of yourself.

I am enough just the way I am.

You are more than enough just the way you are. You don't need to change anything about yourself to be worthy of love and acceptance. Embrace your uniqueness and celebrate who you are.

Personalize it: But have there been times when you felt like you weren't good enough? What happened, and how did you work through those feelings? Write it down.

_____

_____

_____

_____

_____

_____

_____

_____

_____

Put it into practice: Believe in yourself and your worth. Don't compare yourself to others; don't let anyone make you feel inferior. Celebrate your unique qualities and embrace your individuality.

I am a valuable and important
member of my community.

You are a valuable and important member of your community. You bring your own unique talents and perspective to the table, and your contributions make a difference. Keep shining your light and making the world a better place.

Personalize it: Can you think of a time when you feel less of yourself as a community member? What was going on, and how did you work through those feelings? Write it down.

Put it into practice: Get involved in your community and find ways to give back. Volunteer, participate in community events, and support local businesses.

I am worthy of forgiveness and second chances.

Forgiveness is a powerful thing, and you are worthy of it. Remember that we all make mistakes, and it's never too late to learn from them and try again. Give yourself permission to move forward with a clean slate.

Personalize it: Can you think of a time when you struggled to forgive someone or when you struggled to be forgiven? What happened, and how did you work through those feelings?

_____

_____

_____

_____

_____

_____

_____

_____

_____

Put it into practice: Learn from your mistakes, and don't be too hard on yourself. Forgive yourself and others, and give yourself and others a second chance.

I am worthy of love, kindness, and compassion.

You are worthy of love, kindness, and compassion. Don't ever forget that. You deserve to be treated with respect and care by yourself and others. So be kind to yourself, and don't settle for anything less than the love you deserve.

Personalize it: Can you think of a time when you didn't believe you deserved something good? What was holding you back? Write it down.

_____

_____

_____

_____

_____

_____

_____

_____

_____

Put it into practice: Treat yourself and others with kindness, compassion, and love. Focus on building positive relationships and surround yourself with people who uplift and support you.

I trust in my ability to handle difficult situations.

You are strong, resilient, and resourceful. You have everything you need to handle difficult situations. Trust in your own abilities, and know that you are capable of overcoming any challenge that comes your way.

Personalize it: Can you think of a time when you didn't trust yourself to handle something difficult? What happened, and how did you work through those feelings? Write it down.

_____

_____

_____

_____

_____

_____

_____

_____

_____

_____

_____

Put it into practice: Believe in yourself and your ability to handle challenges. Don't be afraid to ask for help when needed, but trust that you have the strength and resilience to overcome difficult situations.

I am worthy of taking up space and speaking my mind.

You are worthy of taking up space and speaking your mind. Your voice matters, and your perspective is essential. Don't let anyone make you feel small or insignificant. Stand tall and be proud of who you are.

Personalize it: But have there been times when you felt like you couldn't do that? What happened, and how did you work through those feelings? Write it down, and let's work on replacing those negative thoughts with positive ones.

_____

_____

_____

_____

_____

_____

_____

_____

_____

_____

Put it into practice: Speak up for yourself and others, and don't be afraid to take up space. Your voice matters, and your opinions are valuable.

I am confident in my skin.

You are confident in your skin, which is something to celebrate. Embrace your body and all its imperfections, knowing that they make you who you are. Your confidence is contagious, so keep shining your light for others to see.

Personalize it: But can you think of a time when you struggled with confidence? What was going on, and how did you work through those feelings?

_____

_____

_____

_____

_____

_____

_____

_____

_____

_____

Put it into practice: Embrace your body and your physical appearance. Focus on self-care and taking care of your physical and mental health.

I am worthy of rest and self-care.

It's essential to take time for yourself and recharge your batteries. Don't feel guilty for putting your needs first. You can't pour from an empty cup, so take care of yourself first and foremost.

Personalize it: Have there been times when you didn't prioritize those things or felt guilty for taking care of yourself? What happened, and how did you overcome those feelings?

_____

_____

_____

_____

_____

_____

_____

_____

_____

_____

_____

_____

Put it into practice: Take care of yourself and prioritize your mental and physical health. Rest when you need to, and take time to recharge and rejuvenate.

I have the power to create positive change in the world.

You can create positive change in the world, no matter how small. Your actions and words have a ripple effect that can touch countless lives. So keep spreading love and positivity, and know you are making a difference.

Personalize it: Can you think of a time when you didn't feel like you could make a difference? What happened, and how did you work through those feelings? Write it down.

_____

_____

_____

_____

_____

_____

_____

_____

_____

_____

Put it into practice: Take action to make a difference in the world. Get involved in social justice causes, environmental initiatives, and other positive movements—every small step counts.

I am proud of my accomplishments and achievements.

You should be proud of all your accomplishments and achievements, big and small. Celebrate your successes and acknowledge how far you've come. You deserve to feel proud of yourself and all that you've accomplished.

Personalize it: Write down all your accomplishments so far and think of goals you want to accomplish soon.

_____

_____

_____

_____

_____

_____

_____

_____

_____

_____

Put it into practice: Celebrate your successes and accomplishments, no matter how small they may seem. Reflect on your growth and progress, and continue to strive towards your goals. You are capable of great things!

I am grateful for all the blessings in my life.

Gratitude is a powerful force, and you have so much to be grateful for. When you focus on what you have instead of what you lack, you invite even more abundance into your life. Take time to appreciate all the blessings in your life, big and small.

Personalize it: What are you grateful for today? Write it down.

_____

_____

_____

_____

_____

_____

_____

_____

_____

_____

Put it into practice: Take a few moments every day to appreciate all the blessings you have. It could be as simple as a warm bed, a delicious meal, or a kind friend.

I am worthy of respect and recognition.

Don't ever settle for less than you deserve. Stand up for yourself and your worth, and know that you are worthy of all the good things life offers.

Personalize it: Can you think of a time when you didn't feel like you were getting the respect or recognition that you deserved? What happened, and how did you work through those feelings? Write it down.

_____

_____

_____

_____

_____

_____

_____

_____

_____

_____

_____

_____

Put it into practice: Stand up for yourself and set boundaries when necessary. Remember that your voice and opinions matter.

I am capable of overcoming any obstacle.

Remember, obstacles may seem daunting initially, but they're not unbeatable. Whether it's a difficult exam, a tough sports match, or a personal challenge, you can overcome it. Take a deep breath, believe in yourself, and tackle that obstacle head-on.

Personalize it: Write down a recent challenge you had and what you did to overcome it.

_____

_____

_____

_____

_____

_____

_____

_____

_____

_____

_____

_____

Put it into practice: Believe in yourself and your abilities to find solutions and overcome obstacles.

I am strong enough to face my fears.

It's natural to feel scared or anxious sometimes, but it's important to remember that fear doesn't have to hold you back. You are strong and capable of overcoming whatever scares you. It might not be easy, but it's worth it.

Personalize it: Can you think of a time when you struggled with facing your fears? What happened, and how did you work through those feelings? Write it down.

_____

_____

_____

_____

_____

_____

_____

_____

_____

_____

_____

Put it into practice: You have the power to face your fears and push through them. Take small steps every day to build your confidence and courage.

I deserve success and abundance.

It's easy to fall into the trap of thinking that success and abundance are only for a select few, but that's not true. Believe in yourself and your abilities, and know you can achieve anything you want. You have the potential to achieve great things and experience abundance in all areas of your life.

Personalize it: Have there been times when you didn't feel like you were experiencing those things? What happened, and how did you cope with those feelings? Write it down.

Put it into practice: Believe in your potential and work hard towards your goals. Remember that you deserve to enjoy the fruits of your labor.

I believe in my own abilities to achieve my goals.

Believing in yourself is a crucial ingredient to success. When you have confidence in your abilities, you're more likely to take action toward achieving your goals. Remember, no dream is too big or too small. If you can dream it, you can achieve it.

Personalize it: Can you think of a time when you didn't believe in yourself or your abilities? What happened, and how did you work through those feelings? Write it down.

_____

_____

_____

_____

_____

_____

_____

_____

_____

_____

Put it into practice: Believe in your own abilities and talents. Set realistic goals and work towards them with determination and focus.

I am capable of making a positive impact on the world.

It's easy to feel like you're just one person and that you can't make a difference, but that's not true. Every action, no matter how small, can have a ripple effect that spreads positivity and makes a difference in the lives of others.

Personalize it: Can you think of a time when you didn't know you could make a difference? What happened, and how did you work through those feelings? Write it down.

_____

_____

_____

_____

_____

_____

_____

_____

_____

_____

Put it into practice: You have the power to make a positive impact on the world. Whether volunteering, being kind to others, or speaking up for what's right, every action counts.

I am worthy of support and encouragement.

It's easy to feel alone or that nobody understands what you're going through, but that's not true. You have people in your life who care about you and want to see you succeed. They're there for you, and they want to see you thrive.

Personalize it: Have there been times when you didn't feel you had enough support or encouragement? What happened, and how did you work through those feelings? Write it down.

_____

_____

_____

_____

_____

_____

_____

_____

_____

_____

Put it into practice: Everyone needs support and encouragement sometimes. Reach out to trusted friends or family members when you need a boost. Remember that you are worthy of kindness and care.

I deserve love and acceptance.

Sometimes it can feel like the world tells you that you must change to fit in or be accepted. But the truth is, you are perfect just the way you are.

Personalize it: But can you think of a time when you didn't feel loved or accepted? What happened, and how did you cope with those feelings? Write it down, and let's work on replacing those negative thoughts with positive ones.

_____

_____

_____

_____

_____

_____

_____

_____

_____

_____

_____

Put it into practice: Love and acceptance start from within. Treat yourself with compassion and understanding. Remember that you are unique and special just the way you are.

I am confident in my own unique abilities and talents.

It's easy to compare yourself to others and feel like you don't measure up, but you are unique and talented in your own way. When you're confident in your abilities, you're more likely to achieve your goals and succeed in life.

Personalize it: Write down your strengths and talents.

_____

_____

_____

_____

_____

_____

_____

_____

_____

_____

_____

_____

Put it into practice: You have unique talents and abilities that make you stand out. You have the power to achieve great things. Embrace your individuality and have confidence in yourself.

I am worthy of taking care of my own needs and wants.

Sometimes it can feel like you're supposed to put everyone else's needs before your own, but that's not true. You are important, and your needs and wants matter. It's important to prioritize your well-being and take care of yourself physically and emotionally.

Personalize it: But have there been times when you didn't prioritize yourself and your needs? What happened, and how did you work through those feelings? Write it down.

_____

_____

_____

_____

_____

_____

_____

_____

Put it into practice: You are important and deserve to prioritize your own needs and wants. Take time to care for yourself and pursue activities that bring you joy and fulfillment.

I am capable of handling anything that comes my way.

Life can be unpredictable and sometimes throws challenges your way, but you have the power to overcome them. Remember that you have faced obstacles before and become stronger on the other side. You have the ability to adapt, learn, and grow from any situation.

Personalize it: Can you think of a time when you didn't believe you deserved something good? What was holding you back? Write it down.

_____

_____

_____

_____

_____

_____

_____

_____

_____

_____

Put it into practice: Life can be challenging at times, but you have the strength and resilience to handle anything that comes your way. Trust in your abilities and keep pushing forward.

I am proud of my individuality and uniqueness.

It's okay to stand out and be different from everyone else. It can be tough to embrace your individuality and uniqueness in a world that can sometimes feel like it values conformity. But the truth is, your unique traits and characteristics are what make you special and exciting.

Personalize it: Have there been times when you didn't feel proud of who you are? What happened, and how did you work through those feelings?

_____

_____

_____

_____

_____

_____

_____

_____

_____

_____

Put it into practice: Embrace your quirks and differences, and be proud of who you are.

I am worthy of having healthy and
fulfilling relationships.

Healthy relationships are essential for your overall well-being. They can provide a sense of belonging, companionship, and happiness.

Personalize it: Healthy relationships are so meaningful, and you deserve them! But have there been times when you didn't have healthy relationships? What happened, and how did you learn to cultivate healthier ones? Write it down.

_____

_____

_____

_____

_____

_____

_____

_____

_____

_____

Put it into practice: Remember that you deserve to be treated with respect, kindness, and love. Surround yourself with people who uplift and support you.

I am capable of creating a life that I love.

Getting caught up in what others expect of you or what society deems successful is easy. Think about what brings you joy, what makes you feel fulfilled, and what you're passionate about.

Personalize it: Creating a life that you love is a great goal! What do you want your life to look like in ten years? Write it down.

_____

_____

_____

_____

_____

_____

_____

_____

_____

_____

_____

_____

Put it into practice: You have the power to create a life that you love. Set goals and take action towards achieving them. Don't be afraid to try new things and take risks.

I deserve peace and harmony in my life.

Life can be challenging at times, and it's easy to get caught up in the chaos of everyday life. Take the time to identify what brings you peace and make it a priority in your life.

Personalize it: Peace and harmony are things you definitely deserve! But have there been times when you didn't feel peaceful or harmonious? What happened, and how did you work towards finding those things again? Write it down.

_____

_____

_____

_____

_____

_____

_____

_____

_____

_____

_____

_____

Put it into practice: Take steps to reduce stress and find inner calm. Practice self-care and reflect on the positive things in your life.

I am confident in my own abilities to achieve success.

It's important to remember that success looks different for everyone, so don't compare your journey to others. Focus on your own abilities, set achievable goals, and work hard towards them.

Personalize it: You should feel confident in your abilities to achieve success! But can you think of a time when you didn't feel confident? How did you work towards building your confidence? Write it down, and let's work on replacing those negative thoughts with positive ones.

Put it into practice: Believe in your abilities and trust you can succeed. Stay focused and work hard towards your goals; you'll be amazed at what you can accomplish.

I am worthy of being treated with respect and dignity.

It's important to remember that you have the power to set boundaries and demand respect. Speak up for yourself and let others know how you want to be treated.

Personalize it: You deserve to be treated with respect and dignity! But have there been times when you didn't receive that treatment? What happened, and how did you work towards getting the respect and dignity you deserve? Write it down.

Put it into practice: Respect and dignity are fundamental human rights. Stand up for yourself and don't tolerate mistreatment from others. Don't settle for anything less than being treated with kindness and consideration.

I am capable of making a positive difference in the world.

Don't underestimate the power of your voice, ideas, and actions. Whether it's volunteering at a local organization or spreading awareness about important issues, you have the ability to make a difference.

Personalize it: Can you think of a time when you didn't know you could make a difference? What happened, and how did you work towards making a positive impact? Write it down.

_____

_____

_____

_____

_____

_____

_____

_____

_____

_____

_____

Put it into practice: You have the power to make a difference in the world, no matter how big or small. Volunteer, speak up for what's right, and be a positive force for change.

*I am worthy of living a life filled
with purpose and meaning.*

Don't be afraid to explore your interests and try new things to discover what brings you joy and purpose. You have unique talents and skills that can be used to positively impact the world and bring meaning to your life.

Personalize it: Have there been times when you didn't feel like you were living a purposeful or meaningful life? What happened, and how did you work towards finding your purpose and meaning? Write it down.

_____

_____

_____

_____

_____

_____

_____

_____

_____

Put it into practice: Life is more fulfilling when you have a sense of purpose and meaning. Explore your passions and find ways to contribute to something greater than yourself.

CHAPTER FIVE

AFFIRMATIONS ON SELF-LOVE

I enjoy being active and exercising for my health.

Not only will exercise help you stay physically healthy, but it can also have a positive impact on your mental and emotional well-being. It can reduce stress, boost your mood, and help you feel more confident and capable in all areas of your life.

Personalize it: Have there been times when you haven't been able to follow through with exercising for your mental health? I encourage you to take a moment to reflect on those times and think about what may have caused you to slip up. Write it down.

_____

_____

_____

_____

_____

_____

Put it into practice: Write down your goals, and track your progress as you go.

I love everything about my body and do
my best to maintain its health.

Remember that our bodies come in all shapes and sizes; no "perfect" body type exists. It's okay to have imperfections or things we want to improve upon, but you should never let those things define how you feel about yourself.

Personalize it: Can you think of a time when you struggled to maintain a positive attitude about your body or didn't take care of it in the best way possible? Take a moment to write down any instances where you may have fallen short of your goal to love and maintain your body's health.

_____

_____

_____

_____

_____

_____

_____

_____

_____

Put it into practice: For all these moments, forgive yourself and start prioritizing self-love and self-care!

My smile brightens up the world.

You never know how much of a difference your smile can make to someone who might be having a tough day or going through a difficult time. Your smile can be a ray of sunshine that brightens up their day and reminds them that there is still kindness and goodness in the world.

Personalize it: Have you ever felt like your smile wasn't quite as bright as you'd like it to be? Maybe you were having a hard time or feeling self-conscious about your teeth or appearance. Take a moment to reflect and write them down.

_____

_____

_____

_____

_____

_____

_____

_____

_____

_____

Put it into practice: For all these moments, forgive yourself, share that smile with the world, and brighten up someone's day.

My brown skin is beautiful.

Your skin color is just one part of what makes you who you are, and it's a beautiful part at that. So, embrace your beautiful brown skin and celebrate the unique beauty that it brings.

Personalize it: Have you ever struggled to see the beauty in your brown skin? Have you ever felt like your skin color wasn't "good enough" or that you needed to change it to fit in with certain beauty standards? So, take a moment to reflect and write down any negative thoughts you may have had about your brown skin - and then let's work together to replace them with positive affirmations!

_____

_____

_____

_____

_____

_____

_____

_____

Put it into practice: Embrace your skin tone and share your confidence with others.

I take care of my body, and it takes care of me.

Taking care of your body is important, especially during your teenage years. Your body is going through many changes, and giving it the fuel and rest it needs to thrive is imperative. By eating healthy, getting enough sleep, and exercising regularly, you're setting yourself up for a happy and healthy future.

Personalize it: Write down a few times when you feel you failed to care for your body. Maybe it was staying up too late and not getting enough sleep or skipping breakfast in the morning. Whatever it is, write it down and think about how you could have made a different choice.

_____

_____

_____

_____

_____

_____

_____

_____

_____

Put it into practice: Make a conscious effort to care for your body, and you will reap the benefits of a healthy and happy life!

I feel attractive in every way.

Remember that true beauty comes from confidence and self-love, so keep up the positive self-talk and focus on what makes you feel good about yourself. Whether it's your personality, style, talents, or smile, there's so much to appreciate and celebrate about yourself.

Personalize it: Have you ever had moments where you didn't feel attractive in every way? So my challenge for you is to take a few minutes and write down any moments where you felt like you weren't attractive in every way. Then, think about what caused those feelings and how you can shift your mindset to focus on your unique beauty and strengths.

_____

_____

_____

_____

_____

_____

_____

_____

Put it into practice: When you embrace your unique beauty and strengths, you radiate confidence that others can't help but be attracted to.

*Every day and in every way, my health
is getting better and better.*

Whether choosing healthy foods, being active, getting enough sleep, or practicing self-care, each day is an opportunity to take steps towards a healthier you.

Personalize it: Have you ever had days where you didn't feel like your health was improving? Maybe you didn't eat as healthy as you wanted, skipped a workout, or didn't take care of yourself as well as you could have. Take a few minutes to write down any moments you feel you didn't progress towards your health goals.

_____

_____

_____

_____

_____

_____

_____

_____

Put it into practice: Make a conscious effort to embrace yourself and practice a healthy lifestyle. Choose healthy foods, stay active, and surround yourself with positive people.

I truly love myself in all ways.

Self-Love is a powerful mindset, and it's important to remember that self-love is a journey that takes time and practice. It's not always easy, but it's always worth it.

Personalize it: Write down a few times when you ever had moments where you didn't feel like you truly loved yourself in all ways. Maybe you were self-critical, focused on your flaws, or compared yourself to others.

_____

_____

_____

_____

_____

_____

_____

_____

_____

_____

_____

Put it into practice: You are amazing just the way you are and deserve to treat yourself with love and kindness.

It is wonderful to feel so loved by myself and others.

Some days will be easier than others, but the most important thing is to keep reminding yourself of your worth and treating yourself with love and kindness.

Personalize it: Take a few minutes to reflect on any times when you haven't felt loved by yourself or others. Write down what happened and how it made you feel. Maybe you felt alone or unappreciated, or maybe you were overly critical of yourself.

_____

_____

_____

_____

_____

_____

_____

_____

_____

_____

_____

Put it into practice: Take a moment to appreciate yourself and feel proud.

Loving myself is the greatest love of all.

When we love ourselves, we can show up in the world with confidence and self-assurance. We can pursue our goals and dreams without fear of judgment or failure.

Personalize it: We all have moments when we feel like we've failed ourselves or haven't lived up to our expectations. Take a moment to think about those times you have struggled with loving yourself and write them down.

_____

_____

_____

_____

_____

_____

_____

_____

_____

_____

_____

Put it into practice: Take a moment each day to show yourself some love and appreciation.

Every day and in every way, my self-love is getting better and better.

Self-love is a journey, and every step you take is progress. Each day is a new opportunity to show yourself love and appreciation, even in small ways.

Personalize it: Have you ever felt like you're not good enough or don't love yourself as much as you should? It happens to everyone! I encourage you to write them down and reflect on them.

_____

_____

_____

_____

_____

_____

_____

_____

_____

_____

_____

_____

Put it into practice: Remember, self-love is a journey, and every day is an opportunity to do better and love yourself more.

I accept the person I am today.

It's not always easy to accept ourselves, especially in a world that can be so critical and judgmental. But by accepting who you are, you're allowing yourself to be authentic and genuine. That's something to be proud of!

Personalize it: Can you think of any times when you didn't fully accept the person you are today? Take a moment to reflect and write down those instances. It's okay if it's uncomfortable to think about - acknowledging your mistakes is the first step towards growth and self-acceptance.

_____

_____

_____

_____

_____

_____

_____

_____

_____

Put it into practice: Take a moment to recognize the things you're good at and the qualities that make you unique. Embrace those strengths and use them to your advantage.

I am in charge of my thoughts and don't judge myself.

Remember, our thoughts have a big impact on how we feel and how we perceive the world around us. You're empowering yourself to create a more positive and fulfilling life by taking charge of your thoughts.

Personalize it: Can you think of any instances when you didn't feel in control of your thoughts or when you judged yourself harshly? Take a moment to reflect and write down those instances.

Put it into practice: Take a few minutes each day to check in with your thoughts and observe them without judgment.

I value my worth. I am talented.

You have unique skills and qualities that make you special and valuable. It's important to celebrate those talents and recognize the positive impact they can have on yourself and others.

Personalize it: Recognizing your worth and talents can be difficult at times, and it's okay if you've struggled with it in the past. Can you think of instances when you didn't value your worth or recognize your talents? Take a moment to reflect and write down those instances.

_____

_____

_____

_____

_____

_____

_____

_____

_____

_____

Put it into practice: Take some time to reflect on your achievements, big or small. Write them down, and credit yourself for your hard work and effort.

I am good with who I am and proud of who I am becoming.

It's necessary to recognize that you are a work in progress, and that's okay. You don't have to have everything figured out right now. Be proud of who you are becoming and actively work towards your goals.

Personalize it: Sometimes, it can be difficult to fully embrace the idea of being good with who you are and being proud of who you are becoming. Can you think of any times when you've struggled with this affirmation? Take a moment to reflect and write down those instances.

_____

_____

_____

_____

_____

_____

_____

_____

Put it into practice: Celebrate what makes you different and unique. Instead of trying to fit in with everyone else, embrace your unique qualities and use them to your advantage.

I am becoming the best version of myself.

You have so much potential within you, and by striving to become the best version of yourself, you're unlocking that potential and making the most of your abilities.

Personalize it: Can you think of times when you failed to live up to this affirmation? Maybe it was when you gave up on a goal or didn't try as hard as you could have. Please take a moment to reflect on those instances and write them down.

_____

_____

_____

_____

_____

_____

_____

_____

_____

_____

_____

Put it into practice: Focus on setting achievable goals for yourself, and take small steps towards achieving them every day.

I am worth something and will not let anyone break me down.

It's not always easy to stay strong in the face of negativity or criticism, but remember that you control your thoughts and emotions. You don't have to let anyone else's negativity bring you down. Instead, focus on all the things that make you great and one-of-a-kind. Celebrate your strengths and use them to your advantage.

Personalize it: Have you ever had someone say something hurtful to you, and it got to you? Grab a pen and paper and take a few minutes to reflect and write them down.

Put it into practice: Don't beat yourself up over mistakes or setbacks. Remember, you are worth something, even when you make mistakes.

I am proud of my body because I worked hard for it.

Our bodies are unique, and they deserve to be celebrated. And when we work hard to take care of them, we have every right to feel proud of ourselves.

Personalize it: Has there been a time when you didn't see the progress you were hoping for, or maybe someone made a negative comment about your body that got to you? Grab a pen and paper and take a few minutes to reflect and write them down.

_____

_____

_____

_____

_____

_____

_____

_____

_____

_____

Put it into practice: Celebrate your progress and the strength and endurance you've gained through your hard work.

I take care of myself physically, mentally, and spiritually.

Taking care of yourself physically means making sure that you're getting enough exercise, eating a balanced and healthy diet, and taking care of your hygiene. It's about making sure your body is functioning at its best.

Personalize it: Take a few moments to reflect and write down any times when you may have failed to take care of yourself physically, mentally, or spiritually.

_____

_____

_____

_____

_____

_____

_____

_____

_____

_____

Put it into practice: Start by incorporating some physical activity into your daily routine. This could be something as simple as taking a walk outside, riding your bike, or doing a workout video on YouTube.

I am loved.

Sometimes it can be easy to forget that we are loved, especially when we face challenges or struggles. But I want you to know that there are people in your life who care about you deeply, even if it doesn't always feel that way.

Personalize it: Have there been times when you didn't feel loved or valued? Take a moment to reflect on these moments and write them down.

_____

_____

_____

_____

_____

_____

_____

_____

_____

_____

_____

Put it into practice: Take time to do things that make you happy and feel good about yourself, whether exercising, meditating, reading a good book, or just relaxing and taking a break.

I am handsome.

It can be easy to compare ourselves to others or focus on our flaws, but it's important to remember that we are all unique and beautiful in our own way. Embrace your individuality and the features that make you stand out.

Personalize it: So, can you think of any times when you've doubted your own handsomeness or felt insecure about your appearance? Write down the features you like about yourself.

_____

_____

_____

_____

_____

_____

_____

_____

_____

_____

_____

Put it into practice: It's important to recognize that you are handsome in your own unique way.

My hair is my crown.

Whether your hair is curly, straight, short, or long, it's part of what makes you who you are. So, embrace your natural texture and color and experiment with different styles that make you feel confident and beautiful.

Personalize it: Have you ever felt like you haven't been treating your hair like the crown it deserves? Please take a moment to think about how you may have failed to treat your hair like the crown it is. Write down your thoughts.

_____

_____

_____

_____

_____

_____

_____

_____

_____

_____

_____

Put it into practice: Embrace your unique hair type and texture, and find styles that make you feel confident and beautiful.

I am worthy of love and respect just the way I am.

It's important to embrace your unique qualities and the things that make you special. You don't have to change your identity to be accepted or loved. You deserve to be loved and respected for who you are.

Personalize it: Can you think of any specific situations in your life where you didn't feel loved or respected, even though you deserved it? Take a few minutes to write down those situations and reflect on how you could have better advocated for yourself and your worth.

_____

_____

_____

_____

_____

_____

_____

_____

_____

Put it into practice: Treat yourself with kindness and compassion. Be gentle, and don't beat yourself up over mistakes or shortcomings.

I choose to love and accept myself just as I am.

Choosing to love and accept yourself can be a powerful and transformative decision. It means letting go of negative self-talk and self-judgment and embrace your unique qualities and quirks.

Personalize it: Can you think of any specific situations where you struggled to love and accept yourself just as you are? Take a few minutes to write down those situations and reflect on what you could have done differently to embrace yourself and your unique qualities.

Put it into practice: Celebrate your accomplishments, big or small. Give yourself a pat on the back for a well-done job, and don't forget to acknowledge your hard work and effort.

I am worthy.

Believing in your worthiness and deservingness can be a game-changer. It means letting go of negative self-talk or self-doubt and embracing a positive mindset that encourages you to go after what you want in life.

Personalize it: Can you think of any specific situations where you may have failed to acknowledge your own worth? Take a few minutes to write down those situations.

_____

_____

_____

_____

_____

_____

_____

_____

Put it into practice: Set healthy boundaries. Don't be afraid to say "no" to things that don't align with your values or goals. This shows that you value yourself and your time and that you deserve good things.

I am precisely enough as I am.

Taking care of yourself is a meaningful way to show yourself that you are enough. This could mean getting enough sleep, eating healthy foods, or doing activities that bring you joy and relaxation.

Personalize it: Have there been times when you didn't feel like you were enough? Maybe you felt like you needed to change something about yourself or do better in order to be accepted or loved. Write them down and think about why you felt that way.

_____

_____

_____

_____

_____

_____

_____

_____

_____

_____

Put it into practice: Every day, try to remind yourself that you are enough and worthy just as you are.

I trust myself and my abilities.

Believing in yourself and your abilities is so important when it comes to achieving your goals and dreams. It can be scary to take risks and put yourself out there, but when you trust yourself, you can overcome any obstacles that come your way.

Personalize it: Have there been times when you doubted yourself and didn't trust your abilities? Maybe you gave up on a project or goal because you didn't think you could succeed. Write them down and think about why you felt that way.

_____

_____

_____

_____

_____

_____

_____

_____

_____

Put it into practice: Remember, building self-trust takes time and practice, so be patient with yourself and don't give up.

I am confident in my own skin.

You might face challenges in life that might shake your confidence, but remember that you have the strength and resilience to overcome them. Believe in yourself and your abilities, and you'll see that you can achieve anything you set your mind to.

Personalize it: Can you think of a time when you felt uncomfortable or insecure about your body or appearance? Take a moment to reflect and jot down any specific situations that come to mind.

_____

_____

_____

_____

_____

_____

_____

_____

_____

_____

Put it into practice: Encourage yourself with kind and supportive words instead of criticizing or putting yourself down.

I forgive myself for any mistakes or shortcomings.

It's beneficial to understand that everyone makes mistakes and nobody is perfect. We all have our flaws and shortcomings, and that's okay. It's totally normal. What's important is how we react to those mistakes and shortcomings.

Personalize it: Have you ever found yourself struggling to forgive yourself for a mistake or shortcoming? What happened, and how did you feel about it? Please take a moment to reflect on those mistakes and what you learned from them.

_____

_____

_____

_____

_____

_____

_____

_____

_____

_____

Put it into practice: Whenever you make a mistake or fall short of your own expectations, take a moment to acknowledge your feelings and emotions.

I am proud of who I am and all that I have accomplished.

Remember that every small achievement counts, and it's essential to acknowledge and appreciate yourself for it. Whether it's acing a test, completing a project, or simply being kind to someone, you are making a difference in the world, and it's something to be proud of.

Personalize it: Can you recall when you didn't feel proud of who you are or what you've done? If you can, take a few moments to write down those experiences and reflect on what you learned from them.

_____

_____

_____

_____

_____

_____

_____

_____

_____

Put it into practice: Take some time to reflect on all the things you have accomplished, big or small, and recognize the hard work and effort you put in to achieve them.

I embrace my uniqueness and individuality.

Embracing your individuality means loving yourself for who you are and not being afraid to show the world your true self. So, don't be afraid to be different and stand out from the crowd.

Personalize it: Can you think of a time when you felt uncomfortable with who you were? Maybe you were trying to fit in or conform to someone else's standards. Take a moment to think about it; if you're comfortable, try to write it down.

Put it into practice: Take time to reflect on what makes you unique and special. Maybe it's your talents, interests, or personality traits.

I am kind and compassionate toward myself.

Remember that we all make mistakes, and it's okay to forgive and treat ourselves with kindness. You deserve to be treated with the same love and compassion you give others.

Personalize it: Can you think of a time when you were tough on yourself and didn't show yourself the same level of kindness and compassion you would show a friend? Take a moment to reflect on that experience and jot down some thoughts.

_____

_____

_____

_____

_____

_____

_____

_____

_____

_____

_____

Put it into practice: Be gentle with yourself when things don't go as planned. Remember that making mistakes is a natural part of learning and growing.

I believe in my dreams and aspirations.

Visualize your dreams and aspirations, and imagine yourself achieving them. This will help to keep you motivated and inspired. When we believe in ourselves and our dreams, we open ourselves up to a world of possibilities.

Personalize it: Can you think of a time when you felt discouraged or doubted yourself? Take a moment to reflect and write down that experience and think about how you can use it as a learning opportunity to help you believe in yourself and your dreams even more.

_____

_____

_____

_____

_____

_____

_____

_____

Put it into practice: Don't be afraid to fail because failure is a part of the journey to success. Stay focused and motivated, and before you know it, you'll be living your dreams!

I am capable of achieving anything I set my mind to.

When you set your mind to something and work hard towards it, there's nothing stopping you from achieving it. Don't let fear or self-doubt hold you back. Believe in yourself and your abilities, and you'll be amazed at what you can accomplish.

Personalize it: Can you think of a time when you set a goal for yourself but didn't believe you could achieve it? Did you end up accomplishing the goal? If not, what do you think held you back?

_____

_____

_____

_____

_____

_____

_____

_____

_____

_____

Put it into practice: Don't be discouraged by setbacks or challenges; see them as opportunities to learn and grow.

I am worthy of love and support from others.

It's natural to want love and support from others, but it's also important to remember that you are capable of loving and supporting yourself. You can give yourself the care and attention you need, which can also attract positive relationships and support from others.

Personalize it: Hey there, have you ever felt like you didn't deserve love and support from the people around you? Can you recall a time when you felt that way? I encourage you to reflect on those moments and write them down.

_____

_____

_____

_____

_____

_____

_____

_____

_____

Put it into practice: Practice self-love! It means treating yourself with kindness, care, and compassion and valuing your own needs and feelings just as much as those of others.

I am worthy of love and support from others.

It's natural to want love and support from others, but it's also important to remember that you are capable of loving and supporting yourself. You can give yourself the care and attention you need, which can also attract positive relationships and support from others.

Personalize it: Hey there, have you ever felt like you didn't deserve love and support from the people around you? Can you recall a time when you felt that way?

_____

_____

_____

_____

_____

_____

_____

_____

_____

_____

Put it into practice: Practice self-love! It means treating yourself with kindness, care, and compassion and valuing your own needs and feelings just as much as those of others.

I acknowledge and appreciate my strengths and weaknesses.

Recognizing our strengths can help us build on them while acknowledging our weaknesses can help us identify areas where we can improve.

Personalize it: Have you ever found it difficult to accept your strengths and weaknesses? Can you think of a specific time when you struggled to acknowledge them?

_____

_____

_____

_____

_____

_____

_____

_____

_____

_____

Put it into practice: Take a few moments each day to reflect on your actions and thoughts and identify your strengths and weaknesses.

I choose to focus on the positives in my life.

It's easy to get bogged down by negative thoughts and situations, but by focusing on the positives, you are training your brain to see the good in everything.

Personalize it: Have there been times when you found it difficult to do so? Maybe when you were faced with a tough situation or when things didn't go as planned?

Put it into practice: Take some time each day to think about what you are grateful for in your life. It could be your family, friends, health, or even the fact that you have a roof over your head and food to eat. Think about these things the next time you face challenges.

I take care of myself physically,
mentally, and emotionally.

Taking care of yourself can sometimes feel like a lot of work, but it's worth it. When you prioritize your physical health by getting enough rest, eating well, and staying active, you feel more energized and ready to take on the day.

Personalize it: Take a moment to reflect on any times when you haven't taken care of yourself physically, mentally, or emotionally. Write down what happened, how you felt, and what you could have done differently.

_____

_____

_____

_____

_____

_____

_____

_____

Put it into practice: Every day, prioritize taking care of yourself in each of these areas. Take breaks throughout the day to move your body and get some exercise.

I respect my own boundaries and needs.

Respecting your own boundaries and needs means that you set limits for yourself and communicate those limits to others in a healthy and assertive way. It also means prioritizing your well-being, even if that means saying no to something or someone.

Personalize it: Take a moment to reflect on any times when you haven't respected your own boundaries or needs. Write down what happened, how you felt, and what you could have done differently to respect yourself better.

_____

_____

_____

_____

_____

_____

_____

_____

_____

_____

Put it into practice: Don't be afraid to prioritize yourself and your needs, and don't let others make you feel guilty for doing so.

I let go of negative self-talk and beliefs.

Negative self-talk and beliefs can be damaging to our self-esteem and confidence, so it's vital to let go of them. Remember, you're amazing just the way you are and deserve to believe in yourself.

Personalize it: Can you think of a time when you struggled to accept a situation and engaged in negative self-talk or beliefs about yourself? Take a moment to jot down some notes about that situation and the negative thoughts you had.

_____

_____

_____

_____

_____

_____

_____

_____

_____

_____

Put it into practice: Whenever you catch yourself engaging in negative self-talk or believing negative things about yourself, try to pause and reframe those thoughts in a more positive way.

I am grateful for all that I have and all that I am.

Gratitude is a powerful force that can help shift our focus toward the positive things in our lives. Even when things might feel burdensome or overwhelming, reflecting on what we're grateful for can help us feel more grounded and appreciative of what we have.

Personalize it: Can you think of a time when you felt you didn't have much to be grateful for? Take a moment to write down what happened and how you felt.

_____

_____

_____

_____

_____

_____

_____

_____

_____

_____

Put it into practice: By focusing on the good things in your life, you'll start to train your brain to look for the positive and appreciate the good things around you.

I honor and value my own opinions and beliefs.

It's also okay to change your opinions and beliefs as you grow and learn. Don't be afraid to challenge yourself and explore new ideas, but always stay true to what feels right to you at the moment.

Personalize it: Can you think of a time when you felt pressured to change your opinions or beliefs to fit in with a group or individual? How did that make you feel? Take some time to reflect on any situations where you may have thought you compromised your beliefs and write them down.

_____

_____

_____

_____

_____

_____

_____

_____

_____

_____

Put it into practice: Don't be afraid to share your thoughts and ideas, even if they may differ from others.

I am proud of my accomplishments and achievements.

Take a moment to celebrate your successes and give yourself credit for all your hard work, whether it's getting a good grade on a test or finishing a project.

Personalize it: Have there been times when you didn't feel proud of your accomplishments or failed to accept the situation? If you can think of any instances like this, I encourage you to take a moment to reflect on them and write them down.

_____

_____

_____

_____

_____

_____

_____

_____

_____

_____

Put it into practice: When you reach a goal, take a moment to acknowledge all the hard work you put in to get there and celebrate your success.

I am proud of my accomplishments and achievements.

It's easy to get frustrated with yourself when you don't see progress or results right away. But remember, growth takes time, so be patient with yourself along the way.

Personalize it: Have there been times when you haven't been patient with yourself or your progress? Maybe it was a situation where you struggled to learn a new skill or complete a task. I encourage you to take a moment to reflect on them and write them down.

_____

_____

_____

_____

_____

_____

_____

_____

_____

Put it into practice: One way to practice patience with yourself and your progress is by breaking down your goals into smaller, manageable tasks.

I am open to learning and growing.

As a teenager, you have many opportunities to learn and grow through your studies, hobbies, or relationships with others. Remember that it's okay to make mistakes and that they're a natural part of the learning process.

Personalize it: Have there been any times when you struggled to accept a situation and didn't learn from it? Think about those situations and try to jot them down.

_____

_____

_____

_____

_____

_____

_____

_____

_____

_____

Put it into practice: Take time to think about what you've learned from your successes and failures.

I release any fear and doubts about my future.

Believing in yourself is the first step towards achieving your dreams. It's normal to feel scared or unsure about the future, but it's important not to let those fears control you. Instead, focus on the positive possibilities and opportunities that lie ahead.

Personalize it: List the fears or uncertainties you have about the future. Please take a moment to reflect and let them go. Do not let these fears control you anymore.

_____

_____

_____

_____

_____

_____

_____

_____

_____

_____

_____

Put it into practice: Visualize success. Imagine yourself achieving your goals and living the life you want.

I am capable of overcoming any challenges.

It's important to remember that challenges are a part of life. They can be difficult and scary, but they also provide opportunities for growth and learning. By believing in yourself and your ability to overcome any challenge, you can face them head-on and come out stronger on the other side.

Personalize it: Can you think of any times when you felt like giving up because you didn't know you could overcome a challenge? Take a moment to note these situations and consider what thoughts or beliefs held you back from overcoming the challenge.

Put it into practice: Challenge yourself to try new things and step out of your comfort zone. Start small and work your way up to more significant challenges.

I deserve love and kindness from myself and others.

It's easy to forget this affirmation and fall into negative self-talk or surround ourselves with people who don't treat us with the respect and kindness we deserve. But remember, you are worthy of love and compassion simply because you exist.

Personalize it: Can you think of any situations where you didn't treat yourself with kindness or allowed others to treat you poorly? Maybe it was a toxic friendship or a negative self-talk cycle. Whatever the situation, take a moment to note it down and reflect on how it made you feel.

Put it into practice: When negative thoughts or self-doubt creep in, take a moment to pause and positively reframe your thoughts.

I am worthy of respect and appreciation.

Sometimes we may find ourselves in situations where we don't feel respected or appreciated by others. It's important to remember that we don't have to tolerate this kind of treatment. We are valuable and deserving of being treated with kindness and respect.

Personalize it: Can you think of a time when you may have failed to accept a situation where you were not being treated with respect or appreciation? Take a moment to note it down and reflect on how it made you feel.

_____

_____

_____

_____

_____

_____

_____

_____

_____

_____

Put it into practice: Set boundaries. Identify what behaviors and treatments are acceptable and unacceptable to you, and communicate them clearly to others.

I am in control of my own happiness and well-being.

You deserve to feel happy and healthy, and it's important to remember that you have control over your own life. You get to choose what makes you happy, what you enjoy, and how you care for yourself.

Personalize it: Have you ever had moments where you struggled to accept a situation or felt like your happiness and well-being were out of your control? Take note of those situations and write them down, so you can reflect on what happened and how to improve next time.

_____

_____

_____

_____

_____

_____

_____

_____

Put it into practice: Reflect on how you're feeling and what you need to feel happy and healthy. This can help you identify areas in your life where you may need to make changes or adjustments.

I deserve my own love and attention.

Sometimes it can be easy to get caught up in what others think of us or to focus on pleasing others before ourselves. But at the end of the day, the relationship we have with ourselves is the most important one we'll ever have.

Personalize it: Have there been times when you didn't believe that you deserved your own love and attention? Take note of those situations and write them down.

_____

_____

_____

_____

_____

_____

_____

_____

_____

_____

_____

Put it into practice: Start by setting aside time each day to focus solely on yourself.

I trust the journey of my life and the lessons it brings

Remember, every experience - both good and bad - can teach us something valuable. Even when things don't go according to plan, trust that there is a lesson to be learned and that you have the strength and resilience to overcome any obstacles that come your way.

Personalize it: Can you think of a time when you struggled to accept a situation or lesson that life brought your way? Take a moment to reflect on that experience and write down how you felt at the time.

_____

_____

_____

_____

_____

_____

_____

_____

_____

_____

Put it into practice: Start by embracing new experiences and challenges, even when they may seem daunting or outside of your comfort zone.

I am grateful for the support and
love I receive from others.

It's important to remember that we don't have to go through life alone; there are people who care about us and want to see us thrive. Whether it's family, friends, teachers, mentors, or even strangers, their support and love can make a huge difference in our lives.

Personalize it: Think back on those times when you may have failed to accept the support and love given to you. Take a few minutes to jot down those experiences and reflect on them.

_____

_____

_____

_____

_____

_____

_____

_____

_____

_____

Put it into practice: Take some time to thank those in your life who you appreciate.

I am capable of creating positive change in my life.

Remember, positive change doesn't always have to be big or drastic. It can start with small, intentional steps toward your goals and aspirations. Whether it's developing a new skill, or taking care of your mental and physical health, every small step counts.

Personalize it: Have there been times when you may have struggled to believe in yourself and your ability to make things happen? Take a few minutes to jot down those experiences.

_____

_____

_____

_____

_____

_____

_____

_____

_____

_____

_____

Put it into practice: Think about what you want to accomplish in your life, whether it's improving your grades, learning a new skill, or building better relationships with others.

I love and respect my body just as it is.

Do you+ know what's cool about loving and respecting your body just as it is? It means that you're accepting yourself for who you are right now instead of constantly striving for some ideal version of yourself that may not even be realistic or healthy.

Personalize it: Can you think of a time when you failed to accept a situation and didn't show love and respect to your body? If you do come up with an example, try writing it down.

_____

_____

_____

_____

_____

_____

_____

_____

_____

_____

Put it into practice: When you catch yourself being hard on yourself or comparing yourself to others, take a deep breath and remind yourself of this affirmation.

I trust in my own decision-making abilities.

Making decisions can be tough, but the more you trust in yourself, the easier it becomes. You know yourself better than anyone else, and you're the best person to make decisions for your own life.

Personalize it: Can you think of a time when you didn't trust yourself to make a decision? Sometimes, we doubt ourselves without even realizing it. But if you take a moment to reflect, you might remember a time when you hesitated to make a decision try writing it down.

_____

_____

_____

_____

_____

_____

_____

_____

_____

_____

Put it into practice: If you ever feel unsure or doubtful, don't hesitate to step back and ask yourself why.

I am deserving of my own forgiveness and compassion.

We all make mistakes from time to time, and it's easy to be hard on ourselves when we do. But it's important to remember that you're only human and that you're allowed to forgive yourself and show yourself compassion.

Personalize it: Can you think of a time when you struggled to forgive yourself or show yourself compassion? If you take a moment to reflect, you might remember a time when you felt guilty, ashamed, or disappointed in yourself. If you do come up with an example, try writing it down.

_____

_____

_____

_____

_____

_____

_____

_____

Put it into practice: Every day, try to show yourself a little bit of forgiveness and compassion.

I choose to focus on the present moment and all its beauty.

Maybe it's the sunshine on your face, the sound of birds chirping, or the taste of your favorite food. Whatever it is, try to take a moment to appreciate it.

Personalize it: Can you think of a time when you were struggling to focus on the present moment and all its beauty? Sometimes, we get so caught up in our thoughts and worries that it's difficult to be present. If you do come up with an example, try writing it down.

_____

_____

_____

_____

_____

_____

_____

_____

_____

_____

_____

Put it into practice: If your mind wanders, that's okay. Gently bring your focus back to your breath and the present moment.

I am deserving of my own time and attention.

It can be easy to get caught up in the demands of daily life and forget to take care of ourselves. But by making time for the things that bring us joy and fulfillment, we can improve our mental and emotional well-being.

Personalize it: Have you ever found yourself putting everyone else's needs and wants before your own? Take some time to write down any situations where you put others first and neglect your own needs.

_____

_____

_____

_____

_____

_____

_____

_____

_____

Put it into practice: Communicate your needs and boundaries with those around you so they understand you're taking time for yourself.

I am confident in my own choices and decisions.

Remember, there will always be people who try to influence your decisions or make you doubt yourself. But it's important to stay true to your own values and beliefs.

Personalize it: Can you think of a time when you made a decision that didn't turn out as planned? How did you feel about it? Take a moment to reflect on that experience and write down any thoughts or feelings that come to mind.

_____

_____

_____

_____

_____

_____

_____

_____

_____

Put it into practice: Don't be afraid to ask for advice or do some research if you need to, but ultimately trust your own judgment and make the decision that feels right for you.

I am worthy of my own self-care and self-love.

It can be easy to forget to take care of ourselves when we're busy with school, friends, and other responsibilities. But it's important to prioritize our own well-being too. By taking care of ourselves, we can show up as our best selves in all aspects of our lives.

Personalize it: Can you recall a time when you neglected your own self-care and didn't give yourself the love you deserved? Take a moment to reflect on that experience and write it down.

_____

_____

_____

_____

_____

_____

_____

_____

_____

_____

Put it into practice: Make it a habit to write down at least one thing you are grateful for each day, and allow yourself to feel the joy and positivity that comes with it.

I am deserving of love and happiness in all areas of my life.

Remember, you are in control of your life, and you have the power to create your own happiness. Focus on the things that bring you joy and surround yourself with positivity. Believe in yourself and your worthiness of love and happiness.

Personalize it: Can you think of a time when you didn't feel deserving of love and happiness in your life? It's okay; we all have those moments. Take a few minutes to reflect on that situation and write down how you felt at the time.

_____

_____

_____

_____

_____

_____

_____

_____

Put it into practice: You are deserving of love and happiness, and you deserve to feel fulfilled and content in all aspects of your life.

I choose to let go of past pain or hurt.

Remember that letting go is a process that may not happen overnight. But with time, patience, and self-compassion, you can release the pain and hurt of the past and move towards a brighter future.

Personalize it: Take a moment to reflect on any past pain you have yet to let go of and write those down.

_____

_____

_____

_____

_____

_____

_____

_____

_____

_____

_____

Put it into practice: It's important to remember that holding onto those feelings can keep us from moving forward and experiencing all the good things life has to offer.

I am capable of achieving my goals and dreams.

Don't let anyone tell you that your goals and dreams are too big or unrealistic. It's critical to have big aspirations, even if they seem impossible right now.

Personalize it: Have you ever experienced a situation where you failed to accept it and just felt like giving up on your goals and dreams? I want to challenge you to take a moment and write down those times when you struggled to accept a situation and felt like giving up.

_____

_____

_____

_____

_____

_____

_____

_____

Put it into practice: It's easy to get overwhelmed by big goals, so breaking them down into small, achievable steps can help you stay focused and motivated.

I am deserving of my own trust and respect.

Remember that you are the main person in your life, and you deserve to treat yourself with kindness, compassion, and respect. That means trusting yourself to make good decisions and being proud of who you are, your flaws, and all.

Personalize it: Have you ever found yourself in a situation where you didn't trust or respect yourself? I want to challenge you to take a moment and write down those times when you didn't trust or respect yourself.

_____

_____

_____

_____

_____

_____

_____

_____

_____

Put it into practice: It's easy to get caught up in what others think of us, but remember that your opinion of yourself is the most important.

I am proud of who I am and all that I have accomplished.

You've worked hard to get where you are today and should be proud of every step you've taken toward your goals. It's easy to focus on our shortcomings and compare ourselves to others, but remember that you are unique and special.

Personalize it: Have there been times when you didn't feel proud of who you are or what you've accomplished?

Put it into practice: Every day, take a moment to reflect on something you're proud of.

I love and accept myself unconditionally.

It's easy to be hard on ourselves and focus on our flaws, but remember that you are unique and special just the way you are. You don't need to change or improve to be worthy of love and acceptance.

Personalize it: Have there been times when you've struggled to love and accept yourself? Write them down and think about why they made you feel the way you did. Maybe it was a time when you made a mistake or didn't live up to your own expectations.

_____

_____

_____

_____

_____

_____

_____

_____

_____

_____

_____

Put it into practice: Pay attention to the things you say to yourself and try to replace any negative self-talk with positive affirmations.

Affirmations for Everyone!

"Life isn't about finding yourself. Life is about creating yourself." – George Bernard Shaw

You're doing great! And now it's time for a moment of reflection.

How are you getting on? Are you noticing a difference in your mindset?

Perhaps you're feeling less stressed and anxious, more empowered to tackle any challenge that comes your way. And that makes sense – there's plenty of science supporting the power of affirmations – at least when you practice them regularly. It's like exercise – you're strengthening your muscles and making yourself stronger every day... but in this case, you're training yourself to become stronger in mind and spirit.

I want as many teenagers as possible to discover the power of affirmations, and now that you're feeling more confident, you're in the perfect position to help me... should you choose to accept the mission! And it's an easy mission – you don't even need to leave your room!

By leaving a review of this book on Amazon, you'll show other young people where they can find all the affirmations they need to become their own superhero.

Simply by letting new readers know how this book has helped you and what they'll find inside, you'll show them where they can find everything they need to improve their confidence and grow stronger by the day.
Scan code below to leave a review.

http://amazon.com/review/create-review?&asin=34571 08552

And if you're looking for something extra yourself, you'll find even more positive affirmations and activities in my other book, The Kid's Guide to Self-Confidence. Scan code below to purchase book.

http://amazon.com/dp/B0C12JXV5D

Thank you for accepting the mission and helping other kids out – it's great to have you on the team!

CHAPTER SIX

AFFIRMATIONS ON RELATIONSHIPS

I am so lucky and blessed in my relationships.

Remember that the relationships with the people in your life are meaningful and can significantly impact your happiness and well-being. Keep nurturing those relationships and valuing those who bring joy and positivity into your life.

Personalize it: Have you ever taken your relationships for granted and not fully realized how lucky and blessed you are to have them? If so, I'd love to hear about it! Take a moment to reflect and write them down.

_____

_____

_____

_____

_____

Put it into practice: Make a list of three things you appreciate about each person in your life that you're close to, and let them know.

I am so blessed to have truly good friends.

You should be proud of yourself for cultivating these friendships and recognizing their value in your life. Not everyone is fortunate enough to have such wonderful friends, so cherish and appreciate them as much as possible.

Personalize it: Can you think of a time when you may have failed to recognize the blessings of your good friends? If so, take a moment to reflect and write them down.

_____

_____

_____

_____

_____

_____

_____

_____

_____

_____

_____

Put it into practice: Think of one thing you can do today to show your appreciation for your good friends.

I take joy in the success and happiness of others.

Celebrating the successes and happiness of others is not always easy, especially when we may be experiencing our own challenges or setbacks. But by choosing to be happy for others, you're cultivating a positive mindset and a heart full of gratitude.

Personalize it: Can you think of a time when you may have failed to celebrate someone else's success or happiness? Take a moment to reflect and write them down.

Put it into practice: The next time someone shares good news or achieves something great, take a moment to celebrate with them.

I wish joy, health, and success to everyone I meet.

When we extend well wishes to others, we create a positive and uplifting environment that benefits them and ourselves. It's a beautiful way to spread kindness and positivity in the world.

Personalize it: Can you think of a time when you may have failed to extend these good wishes to someone you met? Take a moment to reflect on it and write it down.

_____

_____

_____

_____

_____

_____

_____

_____

_____

_____

_____

_____

Put it into practice: When someone tells you about a project they're working on, you can respond by saying, "That sounds great! I wish you success in your endeavors.

I am always fair and just with myself and others.

Remember, being fair and just is not always easy, and sometimes you're faced with difficult decisions or situations. However, staying true to your values and principles allows you to make the right choices and lead a fulfilling life.

Personalize it: Can you think of a time when you may have fallen short of being fair and just with yourself and others.? Take a moment to reflect on it and write it down.

_____

_____

_____

_____

_____

_____

_____

_____

_____

Put it into practice: Always put yourself in the other person's shoes and consider how you would want to be treated if the roles were reversed.

*Every day and in every way, my relationships
are getting better and better.*

Building positive relationships takes time and effort. It's not always easy, but it's worth it in the end. Don't be discouraged if you face obstacles or setbacks along the way. Keep pushing forward and stay committed to making your relationships better every day.

Personalize it: Think about a relationship you wish was better in your life. Was there a time when you could have been more understanding or communicative? Take some time to write down any instances where you feel like you could have done better in that relationship.

Put it into practice: Show up for the people in your life, and try to find ways to bring joy and positivity to their lives.

I am surrounded by amazing friends and family.

Take the time to show your friends and family how much you care about them. Make an effort to spend quality time with them. Listen to their stories, share your experiences, and be there for each other when it matters.

Personalize it: Can you think of a time when you felt like amazing friends and family didn't surround you? Maybe you felt left out of a group or disagreed with someone close to you. Write down what happened and how it made you feel.

_____

_____

_____

_____

_____

_____

_____

_____

_____

_____

Put it into practice: Take a moment to reach out to your friends or family members today and tell them how much you appreciate them.

The more I like myself, the more others will like me.

When we radiate positive energy and confidence, we feel good about ourselves and embrace our unique qualities and strengths. This makes us more attractive to others and can help us form deeper connections with the people around us.

Personalize it: Do you have moments when you struggle with self-doubt or negative self-talk, which can make it hard to love yourself and connect with others? Take a moment to write it down and reflect on what you learned from the experience.

_____

_____

_____

_____

_____

_____

_____

_____

_____

_____

Put it into practice: Think of one thing you can do today to show yourself some love and appreciation.

I have people who care about me and will help me.

Never be afraid to reach out for help or support when you need it. It's not a sign of weakness to ask for help. It takes a lot of strength and courage to admit when you need assistance.

Personalize it: Have you ever had a moment when you felt like you didn't reach out for help when you should have? Whatever it is, take a moment to write it down and reflect on what you could have done differently.

_____

_____

_____

_____

_____

_____

_____

_____

_____

Put it into practice: Think of one thing you're struggling with right now, whether it's a school project or anything else that's weighing on your mind. Then, think of one person in your life who you trust and who you believe can help you with this challenge.

I love and respect my family for all they do for me.

Being a teenager can be challenging at times, but having a supportive family can make all the difference. Your family has likely been there for you through thick and thin, and it's vital to show them the love and respect they deserve.

Personalize it: Have you ever had a moment where you felt like you failed to show your family how much you love and appreciate them for all that they do for you? Please take a moment to think about the times and write them down.

_____

_____

_____

_____

_____

_____

_____

_____

_____

_____

_____

Put it into practice: Think about a tiny thing you can do to show your family how much you love and appreciate them.

I am worthy of love and respect in all my relationships.

You are absolutely deserving of healthy and positive relationships where you are treated with love and respect. Remember that your worth is not determined by what others think of you but by your unique identity.

Personalize it: Have there been times in your relationships when you felt like you weren't being treated with love and respect, but you didn't speak up or take action to change the situation? Write them down.

Put it into practice: By practicing self-love and setting healthy boundaries in your relationships, you can cultivate a life full of love and positivity.

My relationships are healthy and
supportive and bring me joy.

Celebrate the relationships that bring you joy and positivity, and continue cultivating them with care and intention. You deserve healthy, supportive relationships that bring out the best in you.

Personalize it: Have there been times in your relationships when you felt like it wasn't healthy, supportive, or bringing you joy, but you stayed in that relationship anyway? If so, take a moment to think about those situations and write them down.

_____

_____

_____

_____

_____

_____

_____

_____

_____

_____

Put it into practice: Remember that it's okay to prioritize your own well-being in your relationships and to let go of relationships that no longer serve you.

I am open to giving and receiving love in all forms.

By being open to giving and receiving love, you can build meaningful connections with the people around you and create a more positive and supportive environment.

Personalize it: Have there been times in your life when you closed yourself off to giving or receiving love, even if it was offered in a different form than you expected? If so, take a moment to think about those situations and write them down.

_____

_____

_____

_____

_____

_____

_____

_____

_____

_____

_____

Put it into practice: Start by expressing love and appreciation for the people in your life, whether it's through a kind word, a thoughtful gesture, or simply spending quality time together.

I communicate clearly and effectively
in my relationships.

Communication is an essential part of any relationship; when done well, it can create stronger connections and build trust between people.

Personalize it: Have there been times when you struggled to communicate clearly or effectively with someone in your life? Maybe you felt misunderstood, or perhaps you didn't express yourself as clearly as you wanted to. Please take a moment to write them down.

_____

_____

_____

_____

_____

_____

_____

_____

_____

_____

Put it into practice: Start by actively listening to the people in your life and trying to understand their perspective.

I attract positive and loving people into my life.

Surrounding yourself with people who uplift and support you can significantly impact your happiness and well-being. Remember that you deserve to be surrounded by people who bring out the best in you and encourage you to be your authentic self.

Personalize it: Have there been times when you've found yourself attracting negative or unsupportive people into your life, despite your best efforts to surround yourself with positivity? Please take a moment to write them down.

_____

_____

_____

_____

_____

_____

_____

_____

_____

_____

Put it into practice: Start by focusing on being the kind of person you want to attract. Be kind, supportive, and positive in your interactions with others.

I let go of toxic relationships and surround myself with positive energy.

It can be tough to walk away from relationships that no longer serve you, but it's important to remember that you deserve to be surrounded by people who bring out the best in you.

Personalize it: Have there been times when you found it hard to let go of a toxic relationship or felt like you were surrounded by negative energy? What were some of the challenges you faced in trying to move on from those situations? Please take a moment to write them down.

_____

_____

_____

_____

_____

_____

_____

_____

_____

_____

_____

Put it into practice: Practice self-care activities like mindfulness, exercise, or hobbies that bring you joy.

*I trust my instincts and make healthy
choices in my relationships.*

Trusting your gut and making positive choices in your relationships is vital for your well-being and happiness, both now and in the future. Keep it up! Remember that you deserve to be treated with kindness, respect, and love, and don't settle for anything less.

Personalize it: Can you think of any situations in your relationships where you didn't trust your instincts and ended up making an unhealthy choice? Take a moment to reflect.

_____

_____

_____

_____

_____

_____

_____

_____

_____

_____

Put it into practice: Make a conscious effort to listen to your inner voice and prioritize your well-being in your relationships.

*I am committed to growing and
learning from my relationships.*

It's incredible that you're committed to growing and learning
from your relationships. Relationships can be an important
part of our lives and can teach us so much about ourselves and
the world around us.

Personalize it: Take a moment and reflect on your relationships.
What are you doing to grow your relationships, and what have
you learned from them?

Put it into practice: When you're spending time with someone,
make an effort to be fully present in the moment. Put away
distractions like your phone and give the person your full
attention.

*I am confident in expressing my needs
and desires in my relationships.*

When you communicate openly and honestly about what you want and need, you allow the other person to understand and support you.

Personalize it: Can you recall a time when you found it challenging to express your needs or desires to someone you were in a relationship with? Think and ask yourself why it was difficult for you to express yourself. Take some time to write them down.

_____

_____

_____

_____

_____

_____

_____

_____

_____

Put it into practice: When you do express your needs and desires, be as clear and specific as possible. Use "I" statements to communicate your own perspective, and avoid blaming or accusing language.

I forgive myself and others for mistakes in past relationships and move forward with a positive mindset.

Forgiveness can be a powerful tool for healing and growth, both in our relationships with others and in our relationship with ourselves.

Personalize it: Can you tell me about a time when you found it challenging to forgive someone for a mistake they made in a past relationship? Were you holding onto anger or resentment towards them? Take some time to write it down.

Put it into practice: When you're interacting with others, try to put yourself in their shoes and understand where they're coming from.

*I am capable of maintaining healthy
boundaries in my relationships.*

Healthy boundaries help ensure that you treat yourself with
the same care and consideration you show to others. When
you establish boundaries that prioritize your well-being, you
strengthen your relationships by showing that you value yourself
and your needs.

Personalize it: Can you think of a time when you struggled
to maintain healthy boundaries in a relationship? Take note
and write down these situations.

_____

_____

_____

_____

_____

_____

_____

_____

_____

_____

Put it into practice: Every time you successfully set and
maintain a boundary, take a moment to acknowledge and
celebrate that accomplishment.

*I am surrounded by love, understanding,
and compassion.*

You can always seek out new connections and friendships. There are many people in the world who are kind, caring, and empathetic and who would love to have you in their lives.

Personalize it: Have there been a time when you were struggling with a difficult situation and found it hard to accept what was happening? If so, can you think of a specific example and write it down?

Put it into practice: Take a moment each day to reflect on how you can bring more love, understanding, and compassion into your daily activities.

I attract relationships that bring out the
best in me and help me to grow.

It's important to remember that the people we surround ourselves with can have a significant impact on our lives. When we're around people who support, inspire, and encourage us to be our best selves, we're more likely to feel happy, confident, and fulfilled.

Personalize it: Have there been times in your life when you've been in a relationship that didn't bring out the best in you or helped you grow? What happened in those situations? Write it down.

_____

_____

_____

_____

_____

_____

_____

_____

_____

Put it into practice: Look for opportunities to learn from others and to offer your own unique perspective and talents.

I deserve to be in a loving and fulfilling relationship.

As a teenager, it's normal to feel uncertain about relationships and love. But it's important to remember that you are worthy of love and happiness, and you deserve to be in a relationship that makes you feel loved, supported, and fulfilled.

Personalize it: Can you think of a time when you didn't feel like you deserved to be in a loving and fulfilling relationship? What happened in those situations? Write it down.

Put it into practice: Start by treating yourself with love and respect. Take care of your physical and emotional well-being, pursue your interests and hobbies, and spend time with people who uplift and support you.

CHAPTER SEVEN

AFFIRMATIONS ON SUCCESS

I define my success.

It's important to remember that success means something different to everyone. Some people might measure success by their career achievements, while others might measure success by their personal relationships or experiences.

Personalize it: Can you think of a specific instance where you felt like you weren't living up to someone else's definition of success? Take some time to write them down.

_____

_____

_____

_____

_____

_____

_____

Put it into practice: Take some time to reflect on your values, interests, and aspirations.

I am optimistic about the future.

It's natural to have moments of uncertainty and doubt about what the future holds. But it's important to remember that your thoughts and mindset can greatly impact your ability to face challenges and overcome obstacles.

Personalize it: Can you think of a time when you felt pessimistic or negative about the future? Take some time to reflect on this experience and write down your thoughts and feelings about it.

_____

_____

_____

_____

_____

_____

_____

_____

_____

_____

Put it into practice: Take time to do things that make you feel good and help you recharge, like spending time in nature, doing hobbies you enjoy, or practicing mindfulness and meditation.

I can achieve anything I put my mind to.

Remember, achieving your goals and dreams might take time, effort, and hard work, but you can make it happen with persistence and determination.

Personalize it: Have there been times when you felt like you couldn't achieve something, even though you had set your mind to it? Take some time to reflect on those past situations where you might have doubted yourself, and write them down.

_____

_____

_____

_____

_____

_____

_____

_____

_____

Put it into practice: Believe in yourself and your abilities! Remind yourself of this affirmation whenever you doubt yourself or feel like giving up.

I am committed to and productive in
attaining my goals every day.

The key to achieving your goals is to commit yourself to them and be productive every day. Keep your goals in mind and make a plan for how you can work towards them every day.

Personalize it: Can you think of a time when you weren't as committed or productive in working towards your goals as you wanted to be? Please take a moment to reflect on that experience and write down any insights you gained from it that can help you be more committed and productive in the future.

_____

_____

_____

_____

_____

_____

_____

_____

Put it into practice: Make a list of your current goals. Start with small goals, and then write down some goals you want to achieve 5 and 10 years from now. Remember that even if you don't see progress immediately, each small step gets you closer to achieving your goals.

I am committed to self-discipline.

It's great that you are committed to self-discipline! Self-discipline is the key to achieving your goals and becoming the best version of yourself. Even when it's hard, or you face challenges, stay focused and motivated to keep pushing forward.

Personalize it: Have you ever struggled with self-discipline before? What were the circumstances? How did you react to those situations? Take some time to reflect on those experiences and write them down to remind yourself of the importance of self-discipline in achieving your goals.

_____

_____

_____

_____

_____

_____

_____

_____

_____

_____

Put it into practice: Practice makes perfect! Every day is an opportunity to practice self-discipline.

I am open to the opportunities that are around me.

It's important to remember that opportunities come in all shapes and sizes and might not always look like what you expect. But if you keep an open mind and stay curious, you never know what amazing things might come your way.

Personalize it: Can you tell me about a time when you weren't open to a situation and didn't take advantage of an opportunity that was available to you? Take some time to reflect on those experiences and write them down.

_____

_____

_____

_____

_____

_____

_____

_____

_____

_____

Put it into practice: Try something new: Whether it's a new hobby, a new type of food, or a new way of doing things, be open to trying new things. You never know what you might discover!

I inspire and encourage others through my actions.

By being a positive role model and leading by example, you can encourage others to do the same. Whether it's volunteering in your community, helping a friend in need, or simply being kind to those around you, your actions can make a real difference in the world.

Personalize it: Can you think of a time when you might not have lived up to this affirmation? Maybe you missed an opportunity to help someone in need. Take some time to reflect on those experiences and write them down.

_____

_____

_____

_____

_____

_____

_____

_____

Put it into practice: Small acts of kindness can go a long way in making someone's day. Whether it's a smile, a compliment, or an offering to help someone with a task, show kindness to those around you.

I can overcome any obstacle.

When faced with a difficult situation, approach it with a positive attitude and a growth mindset. Focus on what you can learn from the experience, and don't be afraid to ask for help or support when needed.

Personalize it: Can you think of a time when you might not have lived up to this affirmation? Write down what happened. Take a few minutes to reflect on a time when you might not have lived up to this affirmation.

_____

_____

_____

_____

_____

_____

_____

_____

_____

Put it into practice: Setting goals can help you focus your energy and stay motivated when faced with challenges.

*I know there is no such thing as
failure; there is only feedback.*

When you face a setback or make a mistake, try to see it as
feedback rather than failure. Ask yourself what you can learn
from the situation and how you can use that knowledge to
improve in the future.

Personalize it: Can you think of a time when you struggled to
accept a situation that didn't go as planned? Maybe you felt like
you had failed. Take a few minutes to reflect on this situation
and write down what happened.

_____

_____

_____

_____

_____

_____

_____

_____

_____

Put it into practice: When faced with a difficult task or
situation, try to see it as an opportunity to learn and grow rather
than a potential for failure.

Every day and in every way, my success
is getting better and better.

One way to help yourself achieve more remarkable success is to focus on developing good habits and routines. Set small, achievable goals for yourself each day, and make sure to celebrate your accomplishments - no matter how small they may seem.

Personalize it: Can you think of a time when you faced a setback or obstacle that made it hard to believe in your own success? Write down your thoughts and feelings.

_____

_____

_____

_____

_____

_____

_____

_____

_____

_____

_____

Put it into practice: Don't get discouraged by setbacks or failures; instead, view them as opportunities for learning and growth.

I am a successful person.

Success doesn't always mean having achieved everything you want in life. It also means recognizing your strengths and abilities, setting goals for yourself, and taking steps toward achieving them.

Personalize it: Can you think of a time when you faced a difficult situation and felt like a failure? Please take a moment to write it down and then think about how you overcame that challenge.

_____

_____

_____

_____

_____

_____

_____

_____

_____

_____

Put it into practice: Practice positive self-talk and remind yourself that you are capable of achieving your goals.

I am confident and capable of what I do. I believe I can accomplish the goals I am setting for myself.

You should feel proud of yourself for recognizing your capabilities and having the confidence to set goals for yourself. It's important to remember that confidence comes from within and that you have the power to build it up and strengthen it.

Personalize it: Have you ever set a goal for yourself but felt like you couldn't achieve it? What thoughts or beliefs held you back from feeling confident and capable? Take a moment to write it down.

_____

_____

_____

_____

_____

_____

_____

_____

_____

_____

Put it into practice: Keep pushing yourself to learn and grow, and never give up on your dreams.

I take positive actions to make things happen.

Celebrate your victories, no matter how small they may seem, and keep pushing yourself to do more. The more you take action, the more momentum you'll build and the more you'll be able to achieve.

Personalize it: Have you ever found yourself in a situation where you didn't take positive actions and instead let things happen to you? Can you think of a time when you failed to accept the situation and take charge? Take a moment to write it down.

Put it into practice: Challenge yourself to take at least one positive action each day, no matter how small it may seem.

I have an exciting future ahead of me.

So many fantastic opportunities are out there waiting for you to seize them! Keep reminding yourself of the incredible potential you have and the bright future that lies ahead. You are capable of achieving great things, so keep dreaming big and working towards your goals.

Personalize it: Have you ever felt stuck or discouraged about your future? Can you think of a time when you didn't believe you had an exciting future ahead of you? Take a moment to write it down.

_____

_____

_____

_____

_____

_____

_____

_____

_____

Put it into practice: By adopting a mindset of optimism, you can approach each day with a sense of excitement and hope for what's to come.

I am motivated to succeed.

Remember your strengths, passions, and unique talents, and let that motivation fuel your drive toward success. Stay focused on your goals and keep pushing forward even when things get tough.

Personalize it: Can you think of a time when you struggled to feel motivated to succeed? Maybe you felt discouraged or overwhelmed by a particular challenge, and finding the motivation to keep going was hard. Take a moment to write it down.

_____

_____

_____

_____

_____

_____

_____

_____

_____

_____

Put it into practice: Set deadlines, hold yourself accountable, and stay focused on your priorities.

I will always do my best.

Even when faced with challenges or setbacks, continue to put your best foot forward and stay focused on your priorities. Remember, it's not about being perfect or achieving everything right away - it's about giving your best effort and learning from every experience.

Personalize it: Can you think of a time when you struggled to accept a situation and didn't feel like doing your best? Maybe it was a difficult assignment, a tough competition, or a personal challenge that left you feeling discouraged. Take a moment to write it down.

_____

_____

_____

_____

_____

_____

_____

_____

_____

Put it into practice: Every day is an opportunity to show up and do your best, no matter how small the task may seem.

I am going to learn a lot today because I am capable.

Every day is an opportunity to gain new knowledge, develop new skills, and become the best version of yourself. So stay curious, stay open-minded, and don't be afraid to take on new challenges.

Personalize it: Have you ever found yourself in a situation where you didn't feel capable of learning or achieving something new? Maybe you struggled with a subject in school or found a task at work too tricky to tackle. Take a moment to write it down.

_____

_____

_____

_____

_____

_____

_____

_____

_____

Put it into practice: When you wake up in the morning, remind yourself of your own capability to learn and tackle new challenges.

When I get a bad grade, I am motivated to do better.

Instead of getting down on yourself or giving up, use that experience as motivation to do better in the future. Look at where you went wrong and identify areas where you can improve your understanding or study habits.

Personalize it: Have you ever received a bad grade on a test or assignment and felt like giving up? What happened in that situation, and how did you react? Take a moment to write it down.

_____

_____

_____

_____

_____

_____

_____

_____

_____

_____

_____

Put it into practice: Make a plan for improving your study habits and seek help from teachers or tutors if needed.

I am a great student.

You can overcome obstacles and reach your full potential by believing in yourself and your abilities. Celebrate your successes, no matter how small they may seem, and learn from your mistakes to improve continuously.

Personalize it: Have you ever had a moment where you felt like you weren't a great student? Maybe you struggled with a particular subject or didn't perform as well on a test as you had hoped. Take a moment to write it down.

_____

_____

_____

_____

_____

_____

_____

_____

_____

Put it into practice: Practice makes perfect! To become a great student, it's important to consistently work hard and put effort toward your education. Spend time studying the subject or subjects that challenge you.

I study, and I love to learn.

Remember that learning is a lifelong process, and enjoying the journey is essential. Don't put too much pressure on yourself to achieve perfection or to master everything immediately.

Personalize it: Can you think of a time when you faced a setback or challenge in your studies, and you found it difficult to accept the situation? Maybe you were disappointed in yourself, or you felt like giving up. Take a moment to write it down.

_____

_____

_____

_____

_____

_____

_____

_____

_____

_____

_____

Put it into practice: Try to approach every experience as an opportunity to learn something new. Whether you're in class, try to stay open-minded and curious.

I am going to keep working, no matter how hard it gets.

Remember that setbacks and challenges are a normal part of any journey, but they don't have to define your success. Each time you face an obstacle, you have the opportunity to learn and grow from the experience.

Personalize it: Can you think of a time when you faced a difficult situation or challenge, and you found it hard to keep going? Take a moment to write it down.

_____

_____

_____

_____

_____

_____

_____

_____

_____

_____

_____

Put it into practice: Remember that progress doesn't always happen in a straight line, and it's okay to stumble or make mistakes.

Learning new things opens my eyes to new possibilities.

It's amazing that you recognize the power of education and the opportunities it can bring. By keeping an open mind and exploring new topics and ideas, you're expanding your perspective and discovering new pathways you may not have considered before.

Personalize it: Can you think of a time when you were presented with a new idea or opportunity but hesitated to embrace it? Take a moment to reflect on that experience and write it down.

_____

_____

_____

_____

_____

_____

_____

_____

_____

_____

_____

Put it into practice: Challenge yourself to step outside your comfort zone and embrace the unfamiliar.

I am intelligent and capable of learning anything I put my mind to.

Remember, learning is a process, and it's okay to make mistakes along the way. The important thing is to keep a growth mindset and keep pushing yourself to learn and improve.

Personalize it: Can you think of a time when you doubted your own intelligence or ability to learn something new? Maybe you faced a difficult challenge or struggled with a particular subject. Consider jotting down some notes or ideas to help you remember these insights in the future.

_____

_____

_____

_____

_____

_____

_____

_____

_____

_____

Put it into practice: The key is to keep your mind engaged and active and seek new opportunities for growth and learning.

My intelligence and potential are limitless.

It's not just about what you're born with. Your potential is also shaped by your willingness to learn, work hard, and stay focused on your goals. Don't let anyone or anything make you feel like you're incapable of achieving your dreams.

Personalize it: Can you think of a time when you failed to accept a situation and didn't believe in your limitless intelligence and potential?

_____

_____

_____

_____

_____

_____

_____

_____

_____

_____

Put it into practice: Every day, try to find ways to challenge yourself and learn something new. Take on new projects, read books outside of your usual interests, or even try a new hobby.

My future is bright and full of possibilities.

No matter what your dreams and goals are, you have the potential to achieve them. It may not be easy, but with hard work, determination, and a positive attitude, you can accomplish anything you set your mind to.

Personalize it: Can you think of a time when you failed to see the potential in your future and didn't believe it was bright and full of possibilities? Consider jotting them down.

_____

_____

_____

_____

_____

_____

_____

_____

_____

_____

_____

_____

Put it into practice: Your future is yours to create, so take the time to explore all the options and possibilities available to you.

Knowledge will help me succeed.

The more you learn, the more you grow and the more you can achieve. Whether you're interested in science, literature, music, or anything else, there's always something new to discover and learn.

Personalize it: Can you think of a time when you faced a difficult situation and didn't know how to handle it? Maybe it was a tough assignment at school or a personal problem you were struggling with.

Put it into practice: Don't be afraid to ask your teachers, parents, or other experts for advice or information on topics that interest you.

I have the power to create my future.

The choices you make today will impact your future in ways that you might not even realize yet. So take charge of your life and start working towards your goals and dreams.

Personalize it: Can you think of a time when you felt powerless and like your future was out of your control? Maybe it was a situation where you felt stuck or like you had no say in what was happening.

_____

_____

_____

_____

_____

_____

_____

_____

_____

_____

_____

Put it into practice: Cut out pictures and words that represent your goals and dreams, and create a collage that you can look at daily to remind yourself of what you're working towards.

I am going to be successful today.

Believe in yourself and your abilities, and know that you have what it takes to succeed. Whether it's acing a test, nailing a presentation, or just having a positive attitude, there are countless ways for you to achieve success today.

Personalize it: Have there been times when you struggled to believe in yourself or accept a difficult situation? Maybe you received a lower grade than you were hoping for.

_____

_____

_____

_____

_____

_____

_____

_____

_____

_____

_____

Put it into practice: Take a few minutes each morning to set your intentions for the day and write down what you want to accomplish.

I am going to get good grades today.

Start by setting realistic goals for yourself, and break down your tasks into manageable steps. Make a study schedule that works for you, and stick to it as much as possible. Don't forget to take breaks and reward yourself for your hard work.

Personalize it: Have you ever had a time when you didn't do as well as you hoped on a test or assignment and felt disappointed or discouraged?

_____

_____

_____

_____

_____

_____

_____

_____

_____

_____

Put it into practice: One of the keys to getting good grades is being prepared. Make sure you are attending all your classes, taking notes, and completing assignments on time.

I will make it through this exam.

Visualize yourself acing that exam and know that you are capable of achieving great things. Keep focused, take deep breaths, and remember to take breaks to relax and recharge. You will make it through this exam and come out even stronger on the other side.

Personalize it: Can you think of any specific instances where you felt like you failed to accept a situation? Feel free to note and write them down.

_____

_____

_____

_____

_____

_____

_____

_____

_____

_____

Put it into practice: Every day, remind yourself that you have what it takes to succeed and make progress toward your goal.

This test does not define me.

Celebrate your strengths and accomplishments, and don't be too hard on yourself if you don't do as well as you hoped.

Personalize it: Have you ever struggled to accept a situation in the past because you felt like it defined you in some way? Maybe it was a test score, a rejection letter, or a difficult situation at home. Please take a moment to reflect on those instances and write them down.

_____

_____

_____

_____

_____

_____

_____

_____

_____

_____

_____

_____

Put it into practice: Don't let the pressure of upcoming tests and exams consume you. If you make some mistakes on a test or exam, remember what you did wrong and study harder the next time.

My score does not represent my intelligence.

Your score is just one measure of your academic performance, and it doesn't represent your full potential or abilities. You are so much more than just a number; your intelligence extends far beyond what can be measured on a test.

Personalize it: Have you ever received a test score or grade that you felt didn't accurately represent your intelligence or abilities? How did you react to that situation? Take a moment to write them down.

_____

_____

_____

_____

_____

_____

_____

_____

_____

_____

Put it into practice: Don't let a single score discourage you or make you doubt your abilities. Instead, focus on your unique strengths and talents, and keep working hard to achieve your goals.

My best does not have to be the same as anyone else.

Set realistic expectations for yourself, and celebrate your progress and achievements, no matter how small they may seem. Remember that your best is always enough, and moving at your own pace is okay.

Personalize it: Have you ever felt like you had to match someone else's performance or live up to their standards, even if it didn't feel authentic? How did you react to that situation? Take a moment to reflect on those experiences, and write down your thoughts and feelings.

_____

_____

_____

_____

_____

_____

_____

_____

_____

Put it into practice: Don't compare yourself to others or feel like you have to measure up to someone else's expectations.

CHAPTER EIGHT

AFFIRMATIONS ON LIFE IN GENERAL

Life is wonderful and full of opportunity.

It's easy to get caught up in the stress and challenges of daily life, but remember to take a step back and appreciate all the fantastic things that are happening around us.

Personalize it: Have you ever found yourself feeling down or discouraged when faced with a difficult situation or setback? Take a moment to reflect on those experiences, and write down your thoughts and feelings.

_____

_____

_____

_____

_____

Put it into practice: When faced with challenges or setbacks, try to approach them with a positive attitude and an open mind, knowing that every obstacle is an opportunity for growth and learning.

I always find the good in life.

Know that you have an amazing power within you - the ability to find the good in life, no matter what challenges you might face. It's easy to get bogged down by negativity and let it bring us down, but I know that you have the resilience and strength to rise above it.

Personalize it: Have there been times when you've struggled to accept a situation for what it is?

_____

_____

_____

_____

_____

_____

_____

_____

_____

_____

Put it into practice: No matter what challenges you might face throughout the day, try to find something positive about the situation.

Life is full of positive possibilities for me.

Believing that life is full of positive possibilities is such a powerful way to approach the world. When you open yourself up to the idea that good things can happen, you'll be amazed by what you can achieve.

Personalize it: Have there been times when you've struggled to believe that positive possibilities are within reach? Maybe you faced a setback or challenge that made you doubt your ability to achieve your goals. Take a moment to write them down.

_____

_____

_____

_____

_____

_____

_____

_____

_____

_____

Put it into practice: When you wake up in the morning, take a few moments to envision the positive possibilities that the day holds.

I love life. There is so much to love about it.

There's so much to love about life; I'm so glad you recognize that. From the beauty of nature to the joy of spending time with loved ones, there are countless reasons to appreciate and cherish the time you have here.

Personalize it: Have there been times when you've struggled to love life? Maybe you've faced a challenging situation or experienced a setback that made it hard to see the positives. Take a moment to write them down.

_____

_____

_____

_____

_____

_____

_____

_____

_____

_____

_____

Put it into practice: One of the best things about life is that there are so many opportunities to pursue your passions and interests.

I love living and participating in life.

It's important to remember that life is a journey, and there will be ups and downs along the way. But when you love life and actively participate in it, you're better equipped to handle whatever comes your way with grace and resilience.

Personalize it: Have there been times when you found it difficult to love living and participating in life? Maybe there were situations that you found challenging or frustrating. Take a moment to write them down.

Put it into practice: Take time to savor your favorite foods, appreciate the beauty around you, and express gratitude for the people and experiences that bring joy to your life.

I am grateful for everything I have in my life.

When you focus on gratitude, you can also cultivate a sense of contentment and happiness in the present moment. So keep on counting your blessings and appreciating everything that life has to offer.

Personalize it: Have there been times in your life when you found it difficult to feel grateful for what you have? Take a moment to write them down.

_____

_____

_____

_____

_____

_____

_____

_____

_____

_____

_____

_____

Put it into practice: Being grateful is not just a state of mind; it's also an activity that you can practice in your daily life.

Life is kind to me, and I always find my way.

Always trust that no matter what challenges come your way, you have the strength and resilience to overcome them. Believe that life is on your side and wants to help you succeed.

Personalize it: Have there been times when you didn't feel like life was being kind to you or when you struggled to find your way? Maybe you faced a tough challenge at school or had a disagreement with a friend or family member. Take a moment to write them down.

_____

_____

_____

_____

_____

_____

_____

_____

_____

_____

Put it into practice: Resilience means the ability to bounce back from difficult situations and keep moving forward.

*Every day and in every way, my life
is getting better and better.*

I know that life can be tough sometimes, especially when you're going through adolescence and dealing with all kinds of changes and pressures. But I genuinely believe that if you can keep this affirmation in mind and put it into practice, you'll find that things start to feel a little bit easier and more positive.

Personalize it: Have you ever found yourself in a situation where you felt like things were not getting better, no matter how hard you tried?

_____

_____

_____

_____

_____

_____

_____

_____

Put it into practice: Practicing gratitude means taking time to appreciate the good things in your life, no matter how small they may seem.

As I change my thoughts, the life around me changes.

Are you being kind and encouraging to yourself, or are you engaging in negative self-talk? By becoming more aware of your thoughts and beliefs, you can start to challenge negative patterns and replace them with more positive ones.

Personalize it: Have you ever found yourself in a situation where you felt stuck or unhappy? Maybe it was a complicated relationship. Take a moment to write them down.

_____

_____

_____

_____

_____

_____

_____

_____

_____

_____

_____

Put it into practice: Practicing mindfulness means being present and aware of your thoughts and emotions in the present moment. Use positive self-talk to combat any negative thoughts.

Today is going to be a great day.

Whether it's tackling a new project, spending time with friends, or just taking time for yourself, make sure to approach each moment with positivity and gratitude. Remember, you have the power to create a great day for yourself, so go out there and make it happen!

Personalize it: Have there been any times when you woke up feeling down or had a bad start to your day and found it difficult to accept the situation and move forward? Take a moment to write them down.

_____

_____

_____

_____

_____

_____

_____

_____

_____

_____

Put it into practice: If something doesn't go according to plan, don't let it bring you down. Instead, look for ways to turn it around and make the most of the situation.

My life matters; I was created for a purpose.

I know that sometimes it can be hard to see your own worth and purpose, especially when the pressures and stresses of adolescence can make everything seem overwhelming. But trust me when I say that you are here for a reason and that you can make a positive impact on the world around you.

Personalize it: Have you ever found yourself in a situation where you felt like your life didn't matter or like you didn't have a purpose? Take a moment to write them down.

_____

_____

_____

_____

_____

_____

_____

_____

Put it into practice: By working towards your goals, you'll start to see the impact you can have on the world around you.

I am capable of achieving great things.

It's important to remember that greatness doesn't always come easily. It takes hard work, dedication, and sometimes even failure to get to where you want to be. But don't let that discourage you - every setback is an opportunity to learn and grow.

Personalize it: Have you ever found yourself in a situation where you felt like you weren't capable of achieving great things? What did you learn from that experience?

_____

_____

_____

_____

_____

_____

_____

_____

_____

_____

_____

_____

Put it into practice: Trying new things can be scary, but it can also be incredibly enriching and help you discover your strengths and abilities.

I am unique and special, and that is something to celebrate.

Embrace your uniqueness, celebrate your differences, and never try to be someone you're not just to fit in. The world needs you and all that you have to offer. And remember, you are special just the way you are.

Personalize it: Have you ever felt like you needed to change something about yourself in order to fit in or be accepted by others? Maybe you felt like you didn't quite fit in with a particular group of friends; take a moment to write them down.

_____

_____

_____

_____

_____

_____

_____

_____

_____

Put it into practice: You are unique and special, and that is something to celebrate every single day.

I am surrounded by people who love and support me.

You'll feel more confident in yourself and your abilities when you have a strong support system. Remember, you deserve to be surrounded by positive and uplifting people who encourage you to be your best self.

Personalize it: Have you ever been in a situation where you didn't feel supported or loved by those around you? Can you write down what happened and how it made you feel?

_____

_____

_____

_____

_____

_____

_____

_____

_____

_____

_____

Put it into practice: Practice gratitude by acknowledging and expressing appreciation for the people in your life who love and support you.

I have the power to choose my own path in life.

Don't let anyone else dictate your future or make decisions for you. Take control of your life and follow your passions and dreams. Trust yourself and your intuition, and believe that you can achieve anything you set your mind to.

Personalize it: Have you ever felt like your life was out of your control and you didn't have the power to choose your own path? How did you handle that situation, and what did you learn from it?

_____

_____

_____

_____

_____

_____

_____

_____

_____

_____

Put it into practice: Practice autonomy by making conscious choices that align with your values and aspirations and taking ownership of your decisions and actions.

I am confident in my abilities and my worth.

You are unique and special, and there is no one else like you. Celebrate your strengths and talents; don't be afraid to show them off. When you have confidence in yourself, you'll be more successful in all areas of your life.

Personalize it: Have you ever doubted your abilities or felt like you weren't worth as much as others? Can you recall a specific instance and how you overcame those feelings?

_____

_____

_____

_____

_____

_____

_____

_____

_____

_____

Put it into practice: Set realistic goals and take steps towards achieving them, and don't let setbacks or failures discourage you. Remember that you are capable and deserving of success, and believe in yourself and your abilities.

I am open to new experiences and opportunities.

Don't be afraid to try new things and step outside of your comfort zone. You never know what amazing things might happen when you take a chance and try something new.

Personalize it: Have you ever turned down an opportunity because you were afraid of trying something new? Write down what held you back and what you could have gained if you had taken the chance.

_____

_____

_____

_____

_____

_____

_____

_____

_____

_____

_____

Put it into practice: Embrace adventure by trying new things, taking risks, and stepping out of your comfort zone. Seek out opportunities to learn and grow, and approach challenges with a positive and curious mindset.

I am resilient and can overcome any
obstacle that comes my way.

Life can be hard sometimes, but remember you have the strength and resilience to overcome any challenge. Believe in yourself and keep pushing forward, no matter what.

Personalize it: Have you faced a particularly challenging obstacle in your life that you struggled to overcome? Write down what the obstacle was and how you ultimately dealt with it.

_____

_____

_____

_____

_____

_____

_____

_____

_____

_____

Put it into practice: Practice perseverance by facing challenges head-on and not giving up when things get complicated. Break big tasks into smaller, more manageable steps, and celebrate your progress along the way.

*I am deserving of love and respect
from myself and others.*

Treat yourself with kindness and compassion, and set boundaries with people who don't treat you with the respect you deserve. You are worthy of love and affection; don't let anyone tell you otherwise.

Personalize it: Have you ever found yourself in a situation where you felt like you weren't being treated with love or respect? Can you describe how you handled the problem and what you learned from it?

_____

_____

_____

_____

_____

_____

_____

_____

_____

Put it into practice: Practice self-care by setting boundaries and prioritizing your mental, emotional, and physical well-being. Treat yourself with kindness and compassion, and avoid self-criticism or negative self-talk.

I am constantly learning and growing.

The world is full of amazing things to discover and explore, and you have the opportunity to learn and grow every day. Keep an open mind and seek out new knowledge and experiences whenever possible.

Personalize it: Have you ever felt stuck or stagnant in your personal growth? Write down what steps you took to move forward and continue learning.

_____

_____

_____

_____

_____

_____

_____

_____

_____

_____

Put it into practice: Ask questions, challenge assumptions, and be open to new perspectives and ideas. Embrace mistakes and failures as opportunities to learn and grow, and don't be afraid to take risks or try new things.

I have a purpose in life and am
working towards fulfilling it.

Trust the journey and keep taking steps towards your goals and dreams. You can achieve anything you set your mind to, and your purpose is waiting for you to discover it.

Personalize it: Have you ever questioned your purpose in life or felt lost? Can you write down how you found direction and what steps you're taking to fulfill your purpose?

_____

_____

_____

_____

_____

_____

_____

_____

_____

_____

_____

Put it into practice: Break larger goals into smaller, actionable steps, and track your progress along the way. Hold yourself accountable to your goals, and seek out support and guidance from mentors or role models.

I am capable of making a positive
impact on the world around me.

Believe that you are capable of making a positive impact on the world around you, teenager. You have the power to make a difference, no matter how small or large. Whether it's volunteering in your community or standing up for what you believe in, you can make a positive impact on the world.

Personalize it: Have you ever wanted to make a positive impact on the world but didn't know where to start? Write down what actions you've taken or plan to take to make a difference.

_____

_____

_____

_____

_____

_____

_____

_____

Put it into practice: Show kindness and compassion to those around you, and seek to understand and support others who may be struggling. Use your voice and platform to advocate for positive change and work to create a more just and equitable society.

I am worthy of success and happiness.

Remember that you are worthy of success and happiness, teenager. Pursue your dreams and goals with passion and determination, and never give up on yourself. You can achieve anything you set your mind to, and you deserve to be happy and fulfilled in life.

Personalize it: Have you ever felt like you didn't deserve success or happiness? Write down why you felt that way and what steps you can take to change that belief.

_____

_____

_____

_____

_____

_____

_____

_____

Put it into practice: Set boundaries with your time and energy, and make time for activities that bring you joy and fulfillment. Practice self-compassion by treating yourself with kindness and forgiveness and letting go of self-judgment and negative self-talk.

I am in control of my thoughts and emotions.

Remember that it's okay to feel a range of emotions, but it's important to recognize when negative thoughts or feelings are starting to take over. When you notice this happening, try stepping back and focusing on your breath.

Personalize it: Can you think of a time when you felt like your thoughts and emotions were controlling you instead of the other way around? Take some time to reflect on that situation and write down how you felt and what thoughts were going through your mind.

_____

_____

_____

_____

_____

_____

_____

_____

Put it into practice: Try to recognize any negative thoughts that may be affecting your emotions, and challenge them by asking yourself if they're really true or if there's another way to look at the situation.

I am capable of overcoming my fears and doubts.

Don't be too hard on yourself if you have moments of fear or doubt - acknowledge them, but then take action to push through them. You are stronger and more capable than you realize, and with persistence and determination, you can overcome any obstacle in your path.

Personalize it: Can you think of a time when you had doubts about your abilities or felt afraid to try something new? Take a moment to reflect on that experience and write down how you can apply what you learned to overcome future fears and doubts.

_____

_____

_____

_____

_____

_____

_____

_____

_____

Put it into practice: When you feel afraid or doubtful, try to summon your courage and take action anyway. Start with small steps, and gradually work your way up to bigger challenges.

I am confident in my ability to make decisions.

It's also important to recognize that mistakes are a natural part of the decision-making process. Don't be too hard on yourself if you make a choice that doesn't work out as planned.

Personalize it: Can you think of a time when you struggled to accept a situation and found it difficult to make a decision? If so, can you jot down a few notes about what happened and how you felt?

_____

_____

_____

_____

_____

_____

_____

_____

_____

_____

Put it into practice: It's also important to remember that decision-making is a process, and it's okay to take your time to weigh the pros and cons and consider all of your options.

I am kind and compassionate towards myself and others.

Remember that kindness and compassion start with yourself. It's important to treat yourself with the same level of care and understanding that you would offer to a friend. Be gentle with yourself when you make mistakes, and give yourself credit for the things you do well.

Personalize it: Can you think of a time when you found it difficult to show kindness or compassion towards yourself or others? Jot down a few notes about what happened and how you felt.

_____

_____

_____

_____

_____

_____

_____

_____

Put it into practice: When you make a mistake, try not to beat yourself up about it. Instead, recognize that everyone makes mistakes and use them as an opportunity to learn and grow. Be gentle with yourself and give yourself credit for the things you do well.

I am resilient in the face of challenges and setbacks.

What's truly important is how we respond to obstacles. Resilience is all about bouncing back from adversity and continuing to move forward in the face of challenges.

Personalize it: Can you think of a time when you faced a challenge or setback that you found difficult to overcome? If so, can you jot down a few notes about what happened, how you reacted, and how you felt?

_____

_____

_____

_____

_____

_____

_____

_____

_____

_____

Put it into practice: Remind yourself that setbacks are a normal part of life and that you have the strength and resilience to overcome them. Speak kindly to yourself and offer words of encouragement, just as you would to a friend who is facing a difficult situation.

I am worthy of forgiveness and second chances.

Forgiving yourself can be a difficult process, but it's an important step toward growth and healing. Remember that self-forgiveness is not about excusing your actions but rather about accepting responsibility and committing to positive changes in the future.

Personalize it: Can you think of a time when you made a mistake or behaved in a way that you're not proud of? Think about how you could have handled the situation differently. Did you accept responsibility for your actions, or did you try to avoid the consequences?

_____

_____

_____

_____

_____

_____

_____

_____

Put it into practice: Whenever you make a mistake or find yourself in a difficult situation, try to approach yourself with compassion and understanding.

I am proud of who I am and where I come from.

No matter where you come from or what your background is, there is always something to be proud of. Maybe it's your family's heritage or your personal accomplishments, or maybe it's something as simple as your ability to make people laugh or your love of reading.

Personalize it: Have you ever felt like you weren't proud of who you are or where you come from? Maybe you felt like you didn't fit in with your peers, or you didn't like certain aspects of your personality or background. Take a few minutes to write some notes about it.

_____

_____

_____

_____

_____

_____

_____

_____

Put it into practice: Are there aspects of your culture or background that you're particularly proud of? Share that with others, and be open to learning about other people's cultures and backgrounds as well.

I am patient with myself as I work towards my goals.

You got this! Don't compare your progress or timeline to others. Stay focused on your own goals, and be patient with yourself as you work towards them.

Personalize it: Can you think of a time when you felt like giving up on a goal because you were too hard on yourself or didn't see progress as quickly as you wanted to? Did you give up, or did you find a way to be patient with yourself and keep working towards your goal? Take a moment to reflect on that situation and write down what happened, how you felt, and how you responded.

_____

_____

_____

_____

_____

_____

_____

_____

_____

Put it into practice: Keep working towards your goals with patience and perseverance, and you'll get there!

I am excited for what the future holds.

Embrace the excitement and possibilities that come with the future. Think about all the things you're looking forward to, whether it's going to college, starting a new job, traveling, or pursuing your passions.

Personalize it: Can you think of a time when you were feeling down or disappointed about a situation and struggled to feel excited about the future? Maybe it was a rejection from a school or a job, a breakup, or just a difficult period in your life. Write down some positive affirmations and goals for the future to help you stay excited and optimistic about what's to come.

_____

_____

_____

_____

_____

_____

_____

_____

Put it into practice: Keep a positive outlook and look forward to what's to come. Encourage them to take risks, step out of their comfort zone, and try new things.

CONCLUSION

In a world that can be so negative and critical, it is crucial for you, as a young black male, to have access to positive messages that can help boost your self-esteem and confidence.

To all young male teenagers reading this book, I want to remind you that you are strong and capable of achieving anything you set your mind to. Remember to keep reciting the positive affirmations in times of need or when you doubt yourself. You can even get creative and come up with your own affirmations that inspire you.

If you found this book helpful, please consider leaving a review on Amazon. Your feedback will help other young black teen boys find this empowering resource.

Additionally, if you want a free download of positive affirmation cards, please email Tres.Santos.Biz@gmail.com. Let's continue to uplift and support each other on our journey toward success and self-love.

Empower Someone Else!

You can achieve anything you set your mind to, and as you set forward on your journey, you're in a great position to help someone else.

Simply by sharing your honest opinion of this book on Amazon, you'll show other teenagers where they can find all the affirmations they need to empower themselves to reach their own dreams.

MAKE A LASTING IMPRESSION!

Thank you so much for your support. I can't wait to hear about all your successes!

Scan below to leave your review on Amazon.

http://amazon.com/review/create-review?&asin=345710 8552

REFERENCES

100+ Affirmative Sentences in English. (2023). Word Coach. https://www.wordscoach.com/blog/100-affirmative-sentences-in-english/

Aronson, E. (1969). The theory of cognitive dissonance: A current perspective. In L. Berkowitz (Ed.), Advances in experimental social psychology (Vol. 4, pp. 1-34). Academic Press.

Cohen, G. L., Sherman, D. K., Bastardi, A., Hsu, L., & McGoey, M. (2009). Bridging the partisan divide: Self-affirmation reduces ideological closed-mindedness and inflexibility in negotiation. Journal of Personality and Social Psychology, 97(2), 281–291. https://doi.org/10.1037/a0015998

Cohen, G. L., & Sherman, D. K. (2014). The psychology of change: Self-affirmation and social psychological intervention. Annual Review of Psychology, 65, 333-371.

Kotsos, Tania. (2022). Top 100 Positive Affirmations List: Affirmations for the most Important Ares of Life. Mind Your Reality. https://www.mind-your-reality.com/

Martin, Ardis C. MD. (2014). Television Media as a Potential Negative Factor in the Racial Identity Development of African American Youth. Academic Psychiatry volume 32, 338–342 (2008). https://doi.org/10.1176/appi.ap.32.4.338

Quotes about creating yourself. (n.d.). Kids Book Clubs. Subscriptions from Ages 0-12. https: //bookroo.com/quotes/creating-yourself

Riehm KE, et al. (2019). Associations between time spent using social media and internalizing and externalizing problems among US youth. JAMA Psychiatry. doi:10.1001/jamapsychiatry.2019.2325.

Scott, Cheyne. (2021). Affirmation of the Week: I Am Surrounded By People Who Love and Support Me. The Spiritual Litigator. https://www.thespirituallitigator.com/

Sherman, D. K., & Cohen, G. L. (2006). The psychology of self-defense: Self-affirmation theory. Personality and social psychology review, 10(2), 80-97.

Wong, J. (2018). The power of self-affirmation: How to practice self-affirmation for person Affirmations al growth. PositivePsychology.com. Retrieved from https://positivepsychology.com/self-affirmation/

Woods HC, et al. #Sleepyteens: Social media use in adolescence is associated with poor sleep quality, anxiety, depression, and low self-esteem—Journal of Adolescence. 2016; doi:10.1016/j.adolescence.2016.05.008.)

Made in United States
Orlando, FL
22 August 2024

50681745R00157